THE PLANT-BASED BOOST COOKBOOK

100+ Recipes for Athletes and Exercise Enthusiasts

Melissa Halas MA, RDN, CDE

Senior Editor
Claire Haft, MS, RDN

ISBN: 978-1-7339692-1-5

©2019 SuperKids Nutrition Inc.

All Rights Reserved. The information provided in this book is for general informational purposes only. No representations or warranties are expressed or implied about the information, products, services, or related graphics contained in this book for any purpose. No part of this book may be reproduced or transmitted outside of the individual copy sold without written permission of the publisher.

Cover Photo: Danielle Bertiger
Cover Design and Interior Layout: Streetlight Graphics

Table of Contents

Introduction 1

Breakfast 11
- Sweet & Nutty Overnight Oats 13
- Peanut Butter Apple Oats 14
- Ranchero Tofu Scramble 15
- Pea Protein Berry Shake 16
- Zesty Raspberry Protein Smoothie 17
- Pumpkin Spinach Protein Pancakes 18
- Mexican Breakfast Burrito 19
- Very Berry Apple Breakfast Pie 20
- Purple Power Bowl 22
- Crispy Pumpkin French Toast 23
- Chia Acai Bowl 24
- Herby Avocado Toast with Egg or Smoked Salmon 25
- Banana Bread Pancakes 26
- Pineapple Carrot Muffins 27
- Cozy Apple Carrot Streusel Muffin Cups 28
- Mango & Raspberry Yogurt Smoothie Bowl 29
- Eggy Muffin Sandwiches 30
- Herbalicious Cauliflower Egg Cups 31
- Amaranth Breakfast Porridge 32
- Turmeric Egg Scramble 33
- Creamy Dreamy Green Smoothie 34
- Creamy Dreamy Green Smoothie Bowl 35
- Clementine French Toast 36
- Cocoa Berry Yogurt Bowl 37
- Pear Protein Pancakes 38
- Ginger Beet Smoothie 39

Lunch and Dinner 41
- Simple Miso Soup 43
- Herbed Mushroom Barley Soup 44
- Colorful High-Protein Pasta Salad 45
- Chickpea Avocado Salad with Crispy Polenta Croutons 46
- Mediterranean Poached Egg on Toast 47
- Curried Chickpeas 48
- Salsa Autentica Cilantro Tostada 49
- Chile Lime Tempeh Tacos 50
- Black Bean, Corn, and Quinoa Salad 51

Very Veggie Sandwich ... 52
Quick and Easy Farmer's Bowl ... 53
Jackfruit Tacos ... 54
Miso Chopped Salad ... 55
Winter Salad ... 56
Kale Super Salad Bowl ... 57
Middle-Eastern Eggplant Pita ... 58
Walnut Crusted Salmon with Ginger Broccoli ... 59
Roasted Beet, Goat Cheese, and Spinach Salad ... 60
Melissa's Sloppy Joes ... 62
Hearty Sloppy Joes ... 63
TVP Chicken Burgers ... 64
Umami Black Bean Beet Burgers ... 65
Stuffed Pepper with Brown Lentil Salad ... 66
Gallo Pinto Rice ... 67
Marinara Zoodles ... 68
Red Lentil Mac 'n' Cheese ... 69
Mahi Mahi Fish Tacos ... 70
Mushroom Sunflower Seed Burger ... 72
Red Lentil Kabocha Curry ... 74
Ginger Honey Tofu ... 75
Ginger Lime Quinoa Salad ... 76
Farro, Black Beans, and Tofu Bowl ... 77
Sweet Potato Mac 'n' Cheese ... 78
Curried Egg Salad on Millet Bread ... 79
Cumin Tacos with Ginger Broccoli ... 80
Savory Veggie Stew ... 82
Chili Bean Tacos ... 83
Chickpea of the Sea ... 84
Creamy Kale and Potato Soup ... 85
Loaded Baked Potato - Two Ways ... 86
- Mexican Style ... 86
- Savory Brunch Style ... 87
Sweet Potato Nachos ... 88
5-Minute Microwave African Peanut Soup ... 90
Amaranth Veggie Soup ... 91

Snacks/Sides ... 93

Wholesome Homemade Bread ... 95
Spicy Squash Seeds ... 96
Sesame Spinach Sauté ... 97
Ranchy Popcorn Snack ... 98

Mini Egg Frittata	99
"Cheesy" Greens	100
Pea Protein Energy Bars	101
Buttery Corn	102
Hummus Loaded Sweet Potato	103
Hearty Farmer's Market Scones	104
Gluten-Free Hearty Farmer's Market Scones	105
Zucchini Latkes with a Whipped Goat Cheese and Mint Sauce	106
Super Bowl Guacamole	107
Creamed Spinach Artichoke Dip	108
Brussels Sprouts	109
Crispy Sweet Potato Fries	110
Strawberry Oat Scones	111
Moroccan-Style Cauliflower	112
Spiced Sweet Potato Sauté	113
Turmeric Yogurt Dip	114
Cumin Cucumber Rice Cake	115
Fig & Raspberry Ricotta Rice Cake	116
Tahini Chocolate Rice Cake	117
Salted Amaranth Cornbread	118
Creamy Coleslaw	119
Ginger Turmeric Lime Smoothie	120
Tofu Nuggets	121
Apple & Peanut Butter with Whey Shake	122
Edamame Greek Yogurt Dip	123
Tangy and Savory Greek Yogurt Dip	124
Roasted Honey Drizzled Beets	125
Stuffed Dates Three Ways	126

Desserts — 127

Maple Cocoa Brownie	129
Date These Brownies	130
Cocoa Chia Pudding	131
Lemony Blackberry Chia Pudding	132
Graham Cracker Dessert	133
Honey Bee Peanut Butter Cookies	134
Whey Protein Peanut Butter Cookies	135
Sweet & Savory Pumpkin Bowl	136
Blueberry Acai Dessert	137
Chocolate Drizzled Apples	138
Chocolate Chip Oat Protein Bites	139
Tiger Nut Flour Donuts	140

Author Acknowledgements

This book comes with gratitude and praise for Claire Haft's hard work, organization, and drive. The logistics of working on this recipe book while wrapping up the sports nutrition companion book would not have happened without you stepping in whenever and wherever needed. I couldn't have done this without you! Thank you for getting us through the delirium that came with the tedious task of triple checking the nutrition analysis many nights until 10 pm. Your sense of humor somehow made it fun, which had me second-guessing our sanity. You make work enjoyable every day.

Special thanks to Liz Aldridge, Danielle Bertiger and Michelle Rubinstein who helped bring this book to life. From recruiting taste testers of different genders and food preferences to creative ideas and re-photographing timely images, I'm so fortunate to know you all, and I adore each one of you!

Love and thanks to my family and friends for their continual support and for those who served these dishes at gatherings to see which dressings or combinations were received the best! To my good friends, Laura and Jen, whose help with videos to promote the book and constant positivity kept my momentum going. And lastly, thanks to my daughter who let me have the last umami black bean burger tested. I really wanted it, and you let me eat it without making me feel guilty about stealing food from my own child.

About the Author

Melissa Halas, MA, RDN, CDE is a Registered Dietitian Nutritionist, Certified Diabetes Educator, and wellness expert. She has 20 years of diverse experience in nutrition education, nutrition counseling, curriculum development, clinical care, clinical trials, media, and writing. Melissa is the current media representative for the California Academy of Nutrition and Dietetics, the parent nutrition expert for the People.com online magazine, and a past panel expert on Childhood Obesity for TedMed.

Through her company, **Melissa's Healthy Living**, she provides nutrition counseling to help clients of all ages – including athletes – reach their best genetic potential. Melissa believes balanced nutrition contributes to positive spiritual, physical, and mental health. For 18 years she taught functional foods, sports nutrition and other courses, which developed her love for more than one specialty while offering a rewarding and diverse career in nutrition. Melissa is also the founder of **SuperKids Nutrition**, a mega site and premier source for kids and family nutrition, and is the creator of the Super Crew®, a group of multi-cultural characters who get their powers from healthy plant-based foods and motivate young children to develop healthy eating habits from an early age.

INTRODUCTION

I GREW UP EATING KALE, MILLET and a lot of beans. My mom used to say, "I'm adding this for the calcium," and little did I know, her cooking was fueling my love for all things veggie or plant-based. During my college freshman year on the crew team, I didn't have a lot of food choices, and the cafeteria offered mostly meat-based options. At that time, I was studying nutrition, and I began to realize the impact of our food choices on the environment. The diminishing rain forest concerned me, and I remember reading that aspirin was discovered there. Our lifestyle choices directly affect our environment, which in turn poses a barrier to finding future life-saving medicine. Right then, I decided I would eat a more plant-based diet.

We now understand that what we eat significantly impacts the environment. The world's food system is responsible for about one-quarter of the greenhouse gases in our atmosphere. Plant-based eating can positively impact climate change, and it has tremendous benefits for health and longevity. Plant foods are packed with vitamins, minerals, and health-enhancing, disease-fighting phytonutrients. No wonder we hear that boosting plant-based foods is the best thing we can do for our health!

So where does fueling the athlete come into play? I never considered myself to have an athletic physique and running was challenging with my curves. So, in my early 20's, I started cycling. I loved it and saw that sports nutrition played a huge role in my sustained energy and performance with endurance rides. My interest in sports nutrition grew, and shortly after graduate school in my late 20's, I started teaching sports nutrition. I'm still amazed at how significantly food can impact our health – both in the short and long term – for energy, performance, and disease prevention.

Ask yourself, any other athlete, or exercise enthusiast, and I'm sure we'd all agree that we want clean air and water as we enjoy the outdoors! These two elements – air and water – are essential for athletic performance. By adopting sustainable choices, we are helping to ensure that the great outdoors can continue to be our playground. Each person has a unique story, so now that I've shared my plant-based journey, I can't wait to hear yours. Whether you are an expert or a novice in plant-based eating, I hope you enjoy boosting plant-based foods for a fit, long, healthy, and happy life.

SYMBOLS
Look for these symbols if you follow a certain eating style.

PV – pesco-vegetarian

VG – vegetarian

V – vegan

GF – gluten-free (use gluten-free oats when oats are listed)

Recipes may be listed as both vegan and vegetarian. These recipes offer vegan or vegetarian options in the ingredients and/or add-ons.

Many of the recipes can easily be adjusted to be gluten free. Use gluten-free oats when oats are listed. For all other substitutions, you'll find them listed in the recipe introduction.

NUTRITION ANALYSIS
Nutrition software used for nutrition analysis: ESHA Food Processor and USDA Food Composition Databases

Serving Sizes
If the serving size seems small, double or triple it based on your energy needs.

General Measurements
Many recipes use ⅛ teaspoon when a "dash" is indicated. Start out with small amounts of each because you can always add more and work your way up to ⅛ teaspoon!

ABBREVIATIONS AND CONVERSIONS
The following abbreviations will be used with the nutrition analysis:

Tbsp. = tablespoon
tsp. = teaspoon
oz. = ounce

It may also be helpful to know these conversions:
- 1 tablespoon = 3 teaspoons
- 4 tablespoons = ¼ cup
- 2 tablespoons = 1 fluid ounce
- 1 cup = 8 fluid ounces

RECIPE ADD-ONS
Who doesn't like to personalize a recipe? Throughout the book, customize your meals and snacks with these tasty add-ons for a flavor or nutritional boost with added protein, carbohydrate, healthy fats, herbs, and spices. Because they are per

individual taste preferences, most of them are not included on the recipe page analysis. Refer back to add-ons when needed!

Protein Boost
- 6 oz. tofu
- 3 oz. tofu
- ⅓ cup canned white beans
- ½ cup canned black beans
- ¼ cup canned black beans
- 1 medium egg (44g)
- 1 large egg (50g)
- 1 large egg white
- 2 oz. crumbled feta cheese
- 3 oz. chicken breast
- 2 Tbsp. nutritional yeast
- 2 oz. grated parmesan cheese
- 1 oz. grated parmesan cheese
- 2 Tbsp. low-fat shredded cheese
- 2 Tbsp. unsweetened whey protein powder
- 2 Tbsp. unsweetened pea protein powder

Carbohydrate Boost
- ⅓ cup quinoa, GF
- ⅓ cup barley
- ⅓ cup brown rice, GF
- 1 whole-wheat hamburger bun
- Two 4.5" corn tortillas, GF
- 2 hard shell corn tacos, GF
- 1 slice millet bread, GF
- 1 cup Cheerios, GF

Healthy Fat Boost
- ½ small Hass avocado
- ¼ small Hass avocado
- 2 Tbsp. cashews
- 1 Tbsp. almond butter
- 2 Tbsp. roasted peanuts
- 1 Tbsp. peanut butter (creamy)
- 1 Tbsp. peanut butter (chunky)
- 1 Tbsp. flax meal
- 1 Tbsp. chia seeds
- 1 tsp. chia seeds
- 1 Tbsp. hemp seeds
- 2 Tbsp. walnuts (100 Kcals)
- 2¼ Tbsp. sliced almonds (100 kcals)
- 13 whole, dry roasted, unsalted almonds (100 kcals)
- 1 Tbsp. olive oil (extra virgin olive oil is recommended for its higher antioxidant content)

Flavor Boost/Condiments
- 2 Tbsp. crumbled feta cheese
- 2 Tbsp. light sour cream
- 2 Tbsp. lite Mexican cheese
- 2 Tbsp. reduced fat shredded Jack cheese
- 2 Tbsp. vegan cheddar
- 2 Tbsp. caramelized onions
- 2 Tbsp. salsa
- 1 Tbsp. hot sauce
- 1 Tbsp. nonfat vanilla Greek yogurt
- 1 Tbsp. nonfat plain Greek yogurt
- 2 Tbsp. unsweetened shredded coconut
- 1 Tbsp. ketchup
- 1 tsp. spicy brown mustard

- 2 Tbsp. hummus
- 1 Tbsp. Bragg liquid aminos
- 1 tsp. Bragg liquid aminos

Sweet Boost
- ½ cup fresh blueberries
- ½ cup fresh raspberries
- ½ medium banana
- 1 small pear
- 1 sweet, dried plum
- 1 Tbsp. 85% dark chocolate pieces
- 2 Tbsp. maple syrup
- 1 Tbsp. agave
- 1 Tbsp. honey
- 1 tsp. honey
- 1 Tbsp. coconut whipped cream

Phytonutrient Boost – minimal calories
- Vanilla extract
- Cinnamon
- Herbs and spices like chives, cumin, pepper, cayenne
- Lemon and lime juice
- Balsamic vinegar

See our book, *The Plant-Based Boost, Nutrition Solutions for Athletes and Exercise Enthusiasts*, for helpful food tips such as cooking times for grains, and charts for plant-based protein, omega-3s and fiber sources. You'll also get the low-down on phytochemical benefits and how to get more of them in your meals!

PROTEIN BOOST

6 oz. tofu: Kcal 104; Carb 2g; Pro 12g; Fat 6g; Sat. Fat 1g; Fiber 0g; Omega-3 0.4g; Sodium 14mg; Potassium 204mg; Magnesium 46mg; Vit D 0IU; Calcium 189mg; Iron 2mg

3 oz. tofu: Kcal 52; Carb 1g; Pro 6g; Fat 3g; Sat. Fat 0.5g; Fiber 0g; Omega-3 0.2g; Sodium 7mg; Potassium 102mg; Magnesium 23mg; Vit D 0IU; Calcium 95mg; Iron 1mg

⅓ cup canned white beans: Kcal 99; Carb 19g; Pro 6g; Fat 0g; Sat. Fat 0g; Fiber 14; Omega-3 0.1g; Sodium 297mg; Potassium 396mg; Magnesium 45mg; Vit D 0IU; Calcium 64mg; Iron 3mg

½ cup canned black beans: Kcal 113; Carb 20g; Pro 8g; Fat 0g; Sat. Fat 0g; Fiber 7g; Omega-3 0.1g; Sodium 185mg; Potassium 304mg; Magnesium 60mg; Vit D 0IU; Calcium 23mg; Iron 2mg

¼ cup canned black beans: Kcal 57; Carb 10g; Pro 4g; Fat 0g; Sat. Fat 0g; Fiber 4g; Omega-3 0g; Sodium 93mg; Potassium 152mg; Magnesium 30mg; Vit D 0IU; Calcium 12mg; Iron 1mg

1 medium egg (44g): Kcal 63; Carb 0g; Pro 6g; Fat 4g; Sat. Fat 1.5g; Fiber 0g; Omega-3 0g; Sodium 62mg; Potassium 61mg; Magnesium 5mg; Vit D 36IU; Calcium 25mg; Iron 1mg

1 large egg (50g): Kcal 72; Carb 0g; Pro 6g; Fat 5g; Sat. Fat 1.5g; Fiber 0g; Omega-3 0.1g; Sodium 71mg; Potassium 69mg; Magnesium 6mg; Vit D 41IU; Calcium 28mg; Iron 1mg

1 large egg white: Kcal 17; Carb 0g; Pro 4g; Fat 0g; Sat. Fat 0g; Fiber 0g; Omega-3 0g; Sodium 55mg; Potassium 54mg; Magnesium 4mg; Vit D 0IU; Calcium 2mg; Iron 0mg

2 oz. crumbled feta cheese: Kcal 150; Carb 2g; Pro 8g; Fat 12g; Sat. Fat 9g; Fiber 0g; Omega-3 0g; Sodium 520mg; Potassium 191mg; Magnesium 11mg; Vit D 9IU; Calcium 280mg; Iron 0mg

3 oz. chicken breast: Kcal 102; Carb 0g; Pro 19g; Fat 2g; Sat. Fat 0g; Fiber 0g; Omega-3 0g; Sodium 38mg; Potassium 284mg; Magnesium 24mg; Vit D 1IU; Calcium 4mg; Iron 0mg

2 Tbsp. nutritional yeast: Kcal 29; Carb 3g; Pro 4g; Fat 0g; Sat. Fat 0g; Fiber 2g; Omega-3 0g; Sodium 13mg; Potassium 132mg; Magnesium 11mg; Vit D 0IU; Calcium 3mg; Iron 0.5mg

2 oz. grated parmesan cheese: Kcal 238; Carb 8g; Pro 16g; Fat 16g; Sat. Fat 9g; Fiber 0g; Omega-3 0.1g; Sodium 1023mg; Potassium 102mg; Magnesium 19mg; Vit D 12IU; Calcium 484mg; Iron 0mg

1 oz. grated parmesan cheese: Kcal 119; Carb 4g; Pro 8g; Fat 8g; Sat. Fat 4.5g; Fiber 0g; Omega-3 0.1g; Sodium 512mg; Potassium 51mg; Magnesium 10mg; Vit D 6IU; Calcium 242mg; Iron 0mg

2 Tbsp. low-fat shredded cheese: Kcal 44; Carb 0g; Pro 4g; Fat 3g; Sat. Fat 2g; Fiber 0g; Omega-3 0g; Sodium 110mg; Potassium 11mg; Magnesium 4mg; Vit D 2IU; Calcium 100mg; Iron 0mg

2 Tbsp. unsweetened whey protein concentrate powder: Kcal 40; Carb 2g; Pro 7g; Fat 0g; Sat. Fat 0g; Fiber 0g; Omega-3 0g; Sodium 12mg; Potassium 54mg; Magnesium 7mg; Vit D 0IU; Calcium 64mg; Iron 0mg

2 Tbsp. unsweetened pea protein powder: Kcal 47; Carb 0g; Pro 9g; Fat 1g; Sat. Fat 0g; Fiber 0g; Omega-3 0g; Sodium 130mg; Potassium 33mg; Magnesium 0mg; Vit D 0IU; Calcium 17mg; Iron 3mg

CARBOHYDRATE BOOST

⅓ cup quinoa, cooked: Kcal 73; Carb 13g; Pro 3g; Fat 1g; Sat. Fat 0g; Fiber 2g; Omega-3 0.1g; Sodium 4mg; Potassium 105mg; Magnesium 39mg; Vit D 0IU; Calcium 10mg; Iron 1mg

⅓ cup barley, cooked (52g): Kcal 64; Carb 15g; Pro 1g; Fat 0g; Sat. Fat 0g; Fiber 2g; Omega-3 0g; Sodium 2mg; Potassium 49mg; Magnesium 12mg; Vit D 0IU; Calcium 6mg; Iron 1mg

⅓ cup brown rice, cooked (52g): Kcal 82; Carb 17g; Pro 2g; Fat 1g; Sat. Fat 0g; Fiber 1g; Omega-3 0g; Sodium 3mg; Potassium 57mg; Magnesium 26mg; Vit D 0IU; Calcium 2mg; Iron 0.5mg

1 whole-wheat hamburger bun: Kcal 150; Carb 25g; Pro 7g; Fat 2g; Sat. Fat 1g; Fiber 3g; Omega-3 0.1g; Sodium 239mg; Potassium 136mg; Magnesium 45mg; Vit D 0IU; Calcium 111mg; Iron 1mg

Two 4.5" corn tortillas: Kcal 67; Carb 13g; Pro 1g; Fat 1g; Sat. Fat 0g; Fiber 2g; Omega-3 0g; Sodium 7mg; Potassium 0mg; Magnesium 0mg; Vit D 0IU; Calcium 0mg; Iron 0mg

2 hard shell corn tacos: Kcal 100; Carb 13g; Pro 1g; Fat 5g; Sat. Fat 2g; Fiber 1g; Omega-3 0g; Sodium 90mg; Potassium 0mg; Magnesium 0mg; Vit D 0IU; Calcium 13mg; Iron 0mg

1 slice millet bread: Kcal 80; Carb 14g; Pro 5g; Fat 3g; Sat. Fat 0g; Fiber 3g; Omega-3 0g; Sodium 100mg; Potassium 0mg; Magnesium 0mg; Vit D 0IU; Calcium 10mg; Iron 1mg

1 cup Gluten-Free Cheerios (100% whole grain oats): Kcal 100; Carb 20g; Pro 3g; Fat 2g; Sat. Fat 0.5g; Fiber 3g; Omega-3 0g; Sodium 140mg; Potassium 180mg; Magnesium 32mg; Vit D 40IU; Calcium 100mg; Iron 8mg

HEALTHY FAT BOOST

½ small Hass avocado: Kcal 114; Carb 6g; Pro 1g; Fat 10g; Sat. Fat 1g; Fiber 5g; Omega-3 0.1g; Sodium 5mg; Potassium 345mg; Magnesium 20mg; Vit D 0IU; Calcium 9mg; Iron 0.4mg

¼ small Hass avocado: Kcal 57; Carb 3g; Pro 1g; Fat 5g; Sat. Fat 0.5g; Fiber 3g; Omega-3 0g; Sodium 3mg; Potassium 173mg; Magnesium 10mg; Vit D 0IU; Calcium 5mg; Iron 0mg

2 Tbsp. cashews: Kcal 98; Carb 6g; Pro 3g; Fat 8g; Sat. Fat 2g; Fiber 1g; Omega-3 0g; Sodium 3mg; Potassium 97mg; Magnesium 45mg; Vit D 0IU; Calcium 8mg; Iron 1mg

1 Tbsp. almond butter: Kcal 98; Carb 3g; Pro 3g; Fat 9g; Sat. Fat 1g; Fiber 2g; Omega-3 0g; Sodium 36mg; Potassium 120mg; Magnesium 45mg; Vit D 0IU; Calcium 56mg; Iron 1mg

2 Tbsp. roasted peanuts: Kcal 107; Carb 4g; Pro 4g; Fat 9g; Sat. Fat 1g; Fiber 2g; Omega-3 0g; Sodium 1mg; Potassium 116mg; Magnesium 32mg; Vit D 0IU; Calcium 11mg; Iron 0mg

1 Tbsp. peanut butter (creamy): Kcal 96; Carb 4g; Pro 4g; Fat 8g; Sat. Fat 2g; Fiber 1g; Omega-3 0g; Sodium 68mg; Potassium 89mg; Magnesium 27mg; Vit D 0IU; Calcium 8mg; Iron 0.5mg

1 Tbsp. peanut butter (chunky): Kcal 94; Carb 3g; Pro 4g; Fat 8g; Sat. Fat 1g; Fiber 1g; Omega-3 0g; Sodium 78mg; Potassium 119mg; Magnesium 26mg; Vit D 0IU; Calcium 7mg; Iron 0.5mg

1 Tbsp. flax meal: Kcal 35; Carb 2g; Pro 2g; Fat 2g; Sat. Fat 0g; Fiber 2g; Omega-3 2.35g; Sodium 0mg; Potassium 0mg; Magnesium 0mg; Vit D 0IU; Calcium 10mg; Iron 0.5mg

1 Tbsp. chia seeds: Kcal 55; Carb 5g; Pro 2g; Fat 4g; Sat. Fat 0.5g; Fiber 4g; Omega-3 2.1g; Sodium 2mg; Potassium 49mg; Magnesium 40mg; Vit D 0IU; Calcium 76mg; Iron 1.0mg

1 tsp. chia seeds: Kcal 18; Carb 2g; Pro 1g; Fat 1g; Sat. Fat 0g; Fiber 1g; Omega-3 1g; Sodium 1mg; Potassium 16mg; Magnesium 13mg; Vit D 0IU; Calcium 25mg; Iron 0.5mg

1 Tbsp. hemp seeds: Kcal 55; Carb 1g; Pro 3g; Fat 5g; Sat. Fat 0.5g; Fiber 0g; Omega-3 1.1g; Sodium 0.5mg; Potassium 120mg; Magnesium 70mg; Vit D 0IU; Calcium 7mg; Iron 1mg

2 Tbsp. walnuts (100 Kcals): Kcal 100; Carb 2g; Pro 2.5g; Fat 10g; Sat. Fat 1g; Fiber 1g; Omega-3 1.3g; Sodium 0mg; Potassium 64mg; Magnesium 23mg; Vit D 0IU; Calcium 20mg; Iron 0.5mg

2¼ Tbsp. sliced almonds (100 kcals): Kcal 101; Carb 3g; Pro 4g; Fat 8g; Sat. Fat 0.5g; Fiber 2g; Omega-3 0g; Sodium 0mg; Potassium 0mg; Magnesium 0mg; Vit D 0IU; Calcium 45mg; Iron 0.5mg

13 whole, dry roasted, unsalted almonds (100 kcals): Kcal 100; Carb 3g; Pro 4g; Fat 9g; Sat. Fat 0.5g; Fiber 2g; Omega-3 0g; Sodium 1mg; Potassium 119mg; Magnesium 47mg; Vit D 0IU; Calcium 45mg; Iron 0.5mg

1 Tbsp. olive oil: Kcal 120; Carb 0g; Pro 0g; Fat 14g; Sat. Fat 2g; Fiber 0g; Omega-3 0.1g; Sodium 0mg; Potassium 0mg; Magnesium 0mg; Vit D 0IU; Calcium 0mg; Iron 0mg

FLAVOR BOOST/CONDIMENTS

2 Tbsp. crumbled feta cheese: Kcal 50; Carb 1g; Pro 3g; Fat 4g; Sat. Fat 3g; Fiber 0g; Omega-3 0.1g; Sodium 172mg; Potassium 12mg; Magnesium 4mg; Vit D 3IU; Calcium 92mg; Iron 0mg

2 Tbsp. light sour cream: Kcal 40; Carb 2g; Pro 2g; Fat 3g; Sat. Fat 2g; Fiber 0g; Omega-3 0g; Sodium 20mg; Potassium 65mg; Magnesium 0mg; Vit D 0IU; Calcium 60mg; Iron 0mg

2 Tbsp. lite Mexican cheese: Kcal 39; Carb 0g; Pro 3g; Fat 3g; Sat. Fat 2g; Fiber 0g; Omega-3 0g; Sodium 110mg; Potassium 13mg; Magnesium 5mg; Vit D 2IU; Calcium 162mg; Iron 0mg

2 Tbsp. reduced fat shredded Jack cheese: Kcal 20; Carb 0g; Pro 2g; Fat 2g; Sat. Fat 1g; Fiber 0g; Omega-3 0g; Sodium 48mg; Potassium 0mg; Magnesium 0mg; Vit D 0IU; Calcium 63mg; Iron 0mg

2 Tbsp. vegan cheddar: Kcal 80; Carb 6g; Pro 0g; Fat 7g; Sat. Fat 4g; Fiber 0g; Omega-3 0g; Sodium 270mg; Potassium 18mg; Magnesium 0mg; Vit D 0IU; Calcium 237mg; Iron 0mg

2 Tbsp. caramelized onions: Kcal 29; Carb 2g; Pro 0g; Fat 2g; Sat. Fat 1g; Fiber 0g; Omega-3 0g; Sodium 48mg; Potassium 43mg; Magnesium 3mg; Vit D 0IU; Calcium 6mg; Iron 0mg

2 Tbsp. salsa: Kcal 9; Carb 2g; Pro 0g; Fat 0g; Sat. Fat 0g; Fiber 1g; Omega-3 0g; Sodium 228mg; Potassium 88mg; Magnesium 5mg; Vit D 0IU; Calcium 10mg; Iron 0mg

1 Tbsp. hot sauce: Kcal 2; Carb 0g; Pro 0g; Fat 0g; Sat. Fat 0g; Fiber 0g; Omega-3 0g; Sodium 373mg; Potassium 20mg; Magnesium 1mg; Vit D 0IU; Calcium 1mg; Iron 0mg

1 Tbsp. nonfat vanilla Greek yogurt: Kcal 12; Carb 2g; Pro 1g; Fat 0g; Sat. Fat 0g; Fiber 0g; Omega-3 0g; Sodium 4mg; Potassium 13mg; Magnesium 0mg; Vit D 6IU; Calcium 13mg; Iron 0mg

1 Tbsp. nonfat plain Greek yogurt: Kcal 8; Carb 1g; Pro 1g; Fat 0g; Sat. Fat 0g; Fiber 0g; Omega-3 0g; Sodium 5mg; Potassium 15mg; Magnesium 0mg; Vit D 0IU; Calcium 16mg; Iron 0mg

2 Tbsp. unsweetened shredded coconut: Kcal 67; Carb 3g; Pro 1g; Fat 7g; Sat. Fat 6g; Fiber 1g; Omega-3 0g; Sodium 3mg; Potassium 0mg; Magnesium 0mg; Vit D 0IU; Calcium 0mg; Iron 0mg

1 Tbsp. ketchup: Kcal 17; Carb 5g; Pro 0g; Fat 0g; Sat. Fat 0g; Fiber 0g; Omega-3 0g; Sodium 154mg; Potassium 48mg; Magnesium 2mg; Vit D 0IU; Calcium 3mg; Iron 0mg

1 tsp. spicy brown mustard: Kcal 3; Carb 0g; Pro 0; Fat 0g; Sat. Fat 0g; Fiber 0g; Omega-3 0g; Sodium 32mg; Potassium 0mg; Magnesium 0mg; Vit D 0IU; Calcium 0mg; Iron 0mg

2 Tbsp. hummus: Kcal 50; Carb 4g; Pro 2g; Fat 3g; Sat. Fat 0.5g; Fiber 2g; Omega-3 0g; Sodium 114mg; Potassium 68mg; Magnesium 21mg; Vit D 0IU; Calcium 11mg; Iron 1mg

1 Tbsp. Bragg liquid aminos: Kcal 4; Carb 0g; Pro 1g; Fat 0g; Sat. Fat 0g; Fiber 0g; Omega-3 0g; Sodium 960mg; Potassium 0mg; Magnesium 0mg; Vit D 0IU; Calcium 0mg; Iron 0mg

1 tsp. Bragg liquid aminos: Kcal 0; Carb 0g; Pro 0g; Fat 0g; Sat. Fat 0g; Fiber 0g; Omega-3 0g; Sodium 320mg; Potassium 0mg; Magnesium 0mg; Vit D 0IU; Calcium 0mg; Iron 0mg

SWEET BOOST

½ cup fresh blueberries: Kcal 42; Carb 11g; Pro 1g; Fat 0g; Sat. Fat 0g; Fiber 2g; Omega-3 0g; Sodium 1mg; Potassium 57mg; Magnesium 4mg; Vit D 0IU; Calcium 4mg; Iron 0mg

½ cup fresh raspberries: Kcal 30; Carb 8g; Pro 1g; Fat 1g; Sat. Fat 0g; Fiber 4g; Omega-3 0g; Sodium 0mg; Potassium 0mg; Magnesium 14mg; Vit D 0IU; Calcium 20mg; Iron 0.5mg

½ medium banana: Kcal 52; Carb 13g; Pro 1g; Fat 0g; Sat. Fat 0g; Fiber 1g; Omega-3 0g; Sodium 0mg; Potassium 212mg; Magnesium 16mg; Vit D 0IU; Calcium 3mg; Iron 3mg

1 small pear: Kcal 84; Carb 23g; Pro 1g; Fat 0g; Sat. Fat 0g; Fiber 5g; Omega-3 0g; Sodium 1mg; Potassium 172mg; Magnesium 10mg; Vit D 0IU; Calcium 13mg; Iron 0.5mg

1 sweet, dried plum: Kcal 7; Carb 1.5g; Pro 0g; Fat 0.5g; Sat. Fat 0g; Fiber 0g; Omega-3 0g; Sodium 1mg; Potassium 31mg; Magnesium 0mg; Vit D 0IU; Calcium 1mg; Iron 0mg

1 Tbsp. 85% dark chocolate pieces: Kcal 74; Carb 4g; Pro 1g; Fat 6g; Sat. Fat 4g; Fiber 1g; Omega-3 0g; Sodium 0mg; Potassium 81mg; Magnesium 26mg; Vit D 0IU; Calcium 11mg; Iron 2mg

2 Tbsp. maple syrup: Kcal 104; Carb 27g; Pro 0g; Fat 0g; Sat. Fat 0g; Fiber 0g; Omega-3 0g; Sodium 5mg; Potassium 85mg; Magnesium 8mg; Vit D 0IU; Calcium 41mg; Iron 0mg

1 Tbsp. agave: Kcal 64; Carb 16g; Pro 0g; Fat 0g; Sat. Fat 0g; Fiber 0g; Omega-3 0g; Sodium 1mg; Potassium 1mg; Magnesium 0mg; Vit D 0IU; Calcium 0mg; Iron 0mg

1 Tbsp. honey: Kcal 64; Carb 17g; Pro 0g; Fat 0g; Sat. Fat 0g; Fiber 0g; Omega-3 0g; Sodium 1mg; Potassium 0mg; Magnesium 0mg; Vit D 0IU; Calcium 0mg; Iron 0mg

1 tsp. honey: Kcal 21; Carb 6g; Pro 0g; Fat 0g; Sat. Fat 0g; Fiber 0g; Omega-3 0g; Sodium 0mg; Potassium 0mg; Magnesium 0mg; Vit D 0IU; Calcium 0mg; Iron 0mg

1 Tbsp. coconut whipped cream: Kcal 15; Carb 2g; Pro 0g; Fat 1g; Sat. Fat 1g; Fiber 0g; Omega-3 0g; Sodium 0mg; Potassium 0mg; Magnesium 0mg; Vit D 0IU; Calcium 0mg; Iron 0mg

PHYTONUTRIENT BOOST – MINIMAL CALORIES

- Vanilla extract
- Cinnamon
- Herbs and spices like chives, cumin, pepper, cayenne
- Tea
- Lemon and lime juice
- Balsamic vinegar

BREAKFAST

Sweet & Nutty Overnight Oats

I**F YOU'RE LOOKING FOR AN** easy yet wholesome grab-n-go breakfast for those busy mornings, look no further! Make this recipe the night before and stick it in the fridge. No cooking required!

Makes 1 serving

Ingredients:

- ½ cup rolled oats
- ½ cup low-fat milk (or your choice of milk)
- 2 tablespoons walnuts (or swap with other nuts or seeds)
- 1 tablespoon peanut butter (or nut butter of choice)
- ½ cup sliced banana (or substitute fresh or frozen fruit such as berries, bananas, and chopped apples)
- 1 tablespoon ground flaxseed (or chia seeds)
- 1½ tablespoons plain whole Greek yogurt
- Dash of cinnamon and/or cocoa powder

Directions:

1. Combine all ingredients in a jar or bowl. Stir, cover, and refrigerate overnight.
2. In the morning, enjoy chilled oats or reheat for a power-packed start to your day!

Per serving: Kcal 282; Carb 28g; Pro 9g; Fat 16g; Sat. Fat 2g; Fiber 7g; Omega-3 1.6g; Sodium 258mg; Potassium 442mg; Magnesium 96mg; Vit D 110IU; Calcium 580mg; Iron 3g

Peanut Butter Apple Oats

OATS ARE THE PERFECT BLANK canvas for your breakfast. With their mild, creamy taste, and high soluble fiber content, oats epitomize the balance between comfort and health. Beta-glucan, the type of soluble fiber found in oats, has been linked to more modest post-meal glucose increases, as well as decreases in LDL cholesterol – the kind of cholesterol we want less of. Adding flaxseeds or chia seeds is a simple way to further boost your fiber intake while fitting in heart healthy omega-3. You can whip up a nutritious breakfast in minutes that will keep you satisfied for hours!

This is another recipe you can make overnight. Combine all the ingredients in a jar, mix well, and put your jar in the fridge to sit while you sleep! Enjoy cold oats ready to go, or heat for 90 seconds in the microwave.

Makes 1 serving

Ingredients:
- ¼ cup rolled oats
- 1 cup unsweetened almond milk (or water or your choice of milk)
- 2½ tablespoons unsweetened applesauce or grated apple
- 1 tablespoon peanut butter
- 1 tablespoon ground flaxseeds or chia seeds
- 1 teaspoon vanilla extract
- 1 teaspoon cinnamon

Directions:
1. Bring oats and water or milk to a boil.
2. Let simmer for about 10 minutes, stirring occasionally. In the last few minutes of cooking (once a majority of the liquid has been absorbed), stir in apple, peanut butter, ground flaxseeds, vanilla extract, and cinnamon.

Per serving: Kcal 282; Carb 28g; Pro 9g; Fat 16g; Sat. Fat 2g; Fiber 7g; Omega-3 1.6g; Sodium 258mg; Potassium 442mg; Magnesium 96mg; Vit D 110IU; Calcium 580mg; Iron 3g

Ranchero Tofu Scramble

IF YOU'D LIKE THE GLUTEN-FREE version of this scramble choose the taco shells over the whole grain toast. Don't forget to lightly toast the taco shells as it brings out the flavor. You can do this in the toaster oven, or microwave for 20 seconds.

Makes 1 serving

Ingredients:
- 1 cup tofu, soft or medium firmness
- ¼ cup black beans
- ¼ cup diced tomato
- ½ cup fresh spinach
- 1 teaspoon olive oil
- ¼ large Hass avocado
- Dash of salt and pepper
- *Serve with*: 2 toasted corn taco shells for a gluten-free option or whole grain toast

Add-ons: garlic, salt, feta, salsa, hot sauce

Directions:
1. Sauté 1 cup crumbled soft or medium tofu with ¼ cup black beans over medium-low heat.
2. Add in ¼ cup diced tomato, ½ cup fresh spinach, 1 teaspoon olive oil, and season with garlic, salt and pepper.
3. Serve with 2 toasted corn taco shells with avocado on the side, or 1 slice 100% whole grain toast smeared with fresh avocado.

Ranchero Tofu
Per serving: Kcal 377; Carb 25g; Pro 39g; Fat 16g; Sat. Fat 2g; Fiber 16g; Omega-3 0.2g; Sodium 211mg; Potassium 504mg; Magnesium 55mg; Vit D 0IU; Calcium 488mg; Iron 5mg

2 hard shell corn tacos
Per serving: Kcal 100; Carb 13g; Pro 1g; Fat 5g; Sat. Fat 2g; Fiber 1g; Omega-3 0g; Sodium 90mg; Potassium 0mg; Magnesium 0mg; Vit D 0IU; Calcium 13mg; Iron 0mg

Pea Protein Berry Shake

THIS PEA PROTEIN SMOOTHIE MAKES a delicious breakfast or meal any time of day! Use fresh or frozen bananas, berries, and spinach. Adding in the optional nut butter, nuts, seeds, or avocado will pack this smoothie with healthy fats and make it a balanced meal.

Makes 1 smoothie

Ingredients:
- 1 cup unsweetened almond milk
- 1 ripe medium banana
- 1 cup blueberries (or other berries)
- 1 cup raw spinach (or ½ cup frozen, chopped)
- 2 tablespoons (~13g) unflavored pea protein powder

Add-ons: 1 tablespoon nut butter, handful of nuts or seeds, ¼ medium Hass avocado, dash of cinnamon

Directions:
1. Combine ingredients in a blender and mix until smooth.
2. Pour into a glass and enjoy!

Per serving: Kcal 282; Carb 51g; Pro 14g; Fat 5g; Sat. Fat 0g; Fiber 7g; Omega-3 0.2g; Sodium 338mg; Potassium 884mg; Magnesium 79mg; Vit D 110IU; Calcium 573mg; Iron 5mg

Zesty Raspberry Protein Smoothie

THIS FRUIT AND TOFU SMOOTHIE is zingy, creamy, and refreshing. Plus, it's packed with plant-based protein! Silken tofu adds a super creamy texture, and the complex flavors build on your palate. It's sweet from the banana, tart from the raspberries and lime, and has a nice kick from the ginger. The lime cuts the flavor of the tofu; so if you want to pack in even more protein, experiment with adding more tofu with a little extra lime juice.

Makes 1 serving

Ingredients:
- ½ cup silken tofu
- ¼ lime, juiced
- ¾ cup frozen raspberries
- 1 medium fresh or frozen banana
- 1 cup fresh spinach
- 1 teaspoon fresh ginger
- ¾ cup unsweetened soy milk (or your choice of milk)

Directions:
1. Simply blend all ingredients well in a blender. Pour into your favorite glass and enjoy!

Per serving: Kcal 271; Carb 44g; Pro 14g; Fat 7g; Sat. Fat 1g; Fiber 11g; Omega-3 0.2g; Sodium 88mg; Potassium 943mg; Magnesium 103mg; Vit D 0IU; Calcium 354mg; Iron 3mg

Pumpkin Spinach Protein Pancakes

THESE TASTY PANCAKES ARE LOADED with veggies, fiber, and protein to help you start your day with sustained energy. Experiment with different toppings and types of protein powder to find the flavor combo that you like best.

Makes 1 pancake

Ingredients:
- ½ cup raw old-fashioned oats
- ¾ cup liquid egg whites (or 4 egg whites)
- ¼ cup pumpkin puree
- 2 handfuls fresh baby spinach (or 2 ounces)
- 2 tablespoons unsweetened whey protein powder (or unsweetened vegan protein powder)
- 1 tablespoon chia seeds
- Dash of cinnamon or salt

Add-ons: ½ cup fresh or frozen berries, ½ medium banana, 1 tablespoon nut butter or nuts, pinch of salt

Directions:
1. In a blender, combine oats, egg whites, pumpkin puree, spinach (chop if needed), protein powder, chia seeds, ground cinnamon and salt.
2. Lightly oil pan, unless using a non-stick pan.
3. Heat skillet over medium heat while you continue to blend the ingredients until the texture resembles pancake batter.
4. Pour batter into skillet and cook until small bubbles begin to appear. *Tip:* Use a lid to cover the pan to help them cook all the way through.
5. Flip pancake and cook thoroughly on the other side. Your finished pancake will be firm to the touch.
6. Serve with desired toppings and enjoy!

Per serving: Kcal 371; Carb 42g; Pro 36g; Fat 7g; Sat. Fat 1g; Fiber 11g; Omega-3 1.9g; Sodium 362mg; Potassium 671mg; Magnesium 116mg; Vit D 0IU; Calcium 221mg; Iron 5mg

Mexican Breakfast Burrito

DOUBLE OR TRIPLE THIS RECIPE to make some to share or for tasty leftovers for later. It's a colorful, balanced, and nutrient-packed dish that can be enjoyed for lunch or dinner as well.

Makes 1 serving

Ingredients:
- ¼ russet potato
- 3 cremini mushrooms, well cleaned
- ⅓ zucchini
- 2 kale leaves
- 2 teaspoons olive oil
- 1 egg
- ¼ cup shredded lite cheddar cheese (or vegan cheese)
- 2 tablespoons salsa
- 1 whole grain tortilla (or corn tortilla)
- Salt and pepper to taste

Add-ons: ¼ cup pinto or black beans, ½ small Hass avocado, hot sauce

Directions:
1. Dice the potato and cook in a skillet over medium heat. Add ¼ cup water and cover with a lid to speed up the cooking process.
2. While the potato is cooking, dice the zucchini and mushrooms. Add these and the olive oil to the skillet when the potato is almost fully cooked.
3. In a separate bowl, rip the kale into small pieces and scramble with an egg, then add these to the skillet. If adding beans, drain, rinse, and add them to the skillet as well. Let everything cook together until the egg is set and the kale tender.
4. Warm the tortilla, then transfer the skillet mixture and the remaining ingredients to the tortilla. Add cheese, roll up into a burrito, and enjoy!

Per serving: Kcal 418; Carb 39g; Pro 21g; Fat 20g; Sat. Fat 6g; Fiber 7g; Omega-3 0.3g; Sodium 790mg; Potassium 1006mg; Magnesium 92mg; Vit D 37IU; Calcium 329mg; Iron 4mg

Very Berry Apple Breakfast Pie

THIS HEALTHY BREAKFAST PIE IS one you can feel good about starting your day with. It tastes like eating dessert for breakfast, but leaves you feeling energized and ready for any workout on the agenda. This recipe is perfect for a weekend breakfast, or you can make it in the evening so it's ready for a quick grab-and-go breakfast in the morning. This dish also makes a lovely after-dinner treat. It satisfies sweet cravings while also giving you tons of healthy nutrients. It makes getting in those five servings of fruits and vegetables a day a piece of cake... or rather, pie! Serve over a cup of your favorite nonfat Greek yogurt to boost the protein. Make your own gluten-free oats, by blending them in your food processor or blender.

Makes 3 servings

Ingredients:
- 2 medium apples (Fuji, Honeycrisp, or Pink Lady)
- 2 cups frozen mixed berries
- 2 teaspoons cinnamon
- 2 teaspoons honey
- ¼ cup walnuts
- 1 cup granola or homemade oat topping (see granola options)
- 1 tablespoon plain nonfat Greek yogurt
- 1 teaspoon olive oil

Add-ons: 1 tablespoon vanilla nonfat Greek yogurt, 1 tablespoon plant-based whipped cream

Two Granola Options:

Option 1: 1 cup store-bought granola

Option 2: Homemade Crumbled Honey Oats

Homemade Crumbled Honey Oats Ingredients:
- ¾ cup oats
- ¼ cup whole-wheat flour (use oat flour for gluten-free substitution)
- 3 tablespoons olive oil
- 1½ tablespoons honey

Directions:

1. Preheat oven to 350°F and lightly grease a pie dish with olive oil.
2. Thinly slice the apples. If you have a mandolin, use that! Thinly slicing with a knife also works great.
3. Coat apple slices with honey and cinnamon.
4. In alternating layers, place the sliced apples and mixed berries in your pie dish.
5. If you opted for the Homemade Crumbled Honey Oats topping, combine all oat topping ingredients in a medium bowl and mix well, then add this to the top of your pie. If using pre-made granola, add this to the top *after* baking the pie.
6. Bake for 35-45 minutes, or until apples are tender.
7. Remove from the oven and let cool.
8. Put your serving in a bowl, then top with a dollop of Greek yogurt and/or whipped cream and enjoy this tasty morning treat!

Recipe with Granola Option 1
Per serving: Kcal 336; Carb 57g; Pro 6g; Fat 12g; Sat. Fat 1g; Fiber 11g; Omega-3 1.1g; Sodium 19mg; Potassium 340mg; Magnesium 61mg; Vit D 0IU; Calcium 88mg; Iron 2mg

Recipe with Granola Option 2
Per serving: Kcal 537; Carb 76g; Pro 9g; Fat 25g; Sat. Fat 3g; Fiber 13g; Omega-3 0.9g; Sodium 4mg; Potassium 222mg; Magnesium 36mg; Vit D 0IU; Calcium 56mg; Iron 3mg

Purple Power Bowl

(Recipe Credit: Erin Kratzer, MS, RDN, LDN)

> IF BLUEBERRIES AND MULBERRIES AREN'T in season, buy them frozen. Frozen berries are typically picked at peak freshness then frozen to maximize the nutrition profile. The frozen varieties are usually less expensive too!

Makes 2 servings

Ingredients:
- ½ cup fresh blueberries
- ½ cup fresh mulberries
- 1 medium banana
- ½ cup plain low-fat Greek yogurt
- 1 cup fresh baby spinach
- ¼ cup 100% pomegranate juice (or cherry juice)
- ¾ cup water (or 1 cup if using frozen berries)

Directions:
1. Add juice, water, yogurt, and fruits to the blender.
2. Blend on high speed for 30-60 seconds or until mixture runs smoothly and is completely mixed.
3. Pour into two bowls and add your desired toppings.
4. Enjoy!

Add-ons: Pick your favorite super foods such as walnuts, chia seeds, hemp seeds, ground flaxseed, or dark chocolate pieces.

Per serving: Kcal 153; Carb 29g; Pro 8g; Fat 2g; Sat. Fat 1g; Fiber 3g; Omega-3 0g; Sodium 36mg; Potassium 460mg; Magnesium 33mg; Vit D 0IU; Calcium 100mg; Iron 1mg

Crispy Pumpkin French Toast

THIS IS EXTRA TASTY AND crispy on a grill pan.

Makes 4 servings (2 slices of toast per serving)

Ingredients:
- 2 eggs
- 1 cup 2% milk
- 2 teaspoons canola oil
- 2 tablespoons honey
- ½ teaspoon pumpkin pie spice
- 1 teaspoon vanilla extract
- 1 teaspoon cinnamon
- 2 pinches salt
- 4 teaspoons healthy butter substitute
- 8 slices whole grain bread
- 2 tablespoons canned pumpkin
- *Serve with*: 2 tablespoons maple syrup (pour in a small dish and dip your toast)

Directions:
1. Whisk egg, milk, canola oil, honey, canned pumpkin, and vanilla extract in a bowl.
2. Add in the pumpkin pie spice, cinnamon, and salt into the wet ingredients.
3. Place the bread into the egg mixture and make sure both sides are well dipped.
4. Melt 4 teaspoons butter substitute in a pan.
5. Cook 1 minute on each side on medium-low heat until light brown.
6. Dip the toast into egg mixture again.
7. Cook for another minute on each side, until both sides are golden brown.

Per serving: Kcal 337; Carb 44g; Pro 14g; Fat 12g; Sat. Fat 3g; Fiber 5g; Omega-3 0.3g; Sodium 501mg; Potassium 326mg; Magnesium 66mg; Vit D 19IU; Calcium 213mg; Iron 2mg

2 Tablespoons maple syrup
Kcal 104; Carb 27g; Pro 0g; Fat 0g; Sat. Fat 0g; Fiber 0g; Omega-3 0g; Sodium 5mg; Potassium 85mg; Magnesium 8mg; Vit D 0IU; Calcium 41mg; Iron 0mg

Chia Acai Bowl

> IF YOU'RE LOOKING FOR A little extra sweetness, use French Agen plums in this recipe. They're juicy and delicious. Otherwise, any variety will work.

Makes 2 servings

Ingredients:
- ½ cup frozen spinach
- 1 (100g) sweetened frozen acai smoothie packet
- 1 cup frozen blueberries
- ½ cup frozen mango
- 3 tablespoons Meyer lemon juice
- 1 cup unsweetened soy milk
- 1 teaspoon chia seeds
- 1 dried but juicy plum

Add-ons: 1 tablespoon broken dark chocolate pieces

Directions:
1. Measure ingredients and place in blender.
2. Blend together, periodically pausing to hand-mix ingredients with a spoon.
3. Serve in a bowl and add toppings.
4. Enjoy!

Per serving: Kcal 250; Carb 40g; Pro 7g; Fat 8g; Sat. Fat 1g; Fiber 6g; Omega-3 0.4g; Sodium 87mg; Potassium 392mg; Magnesium 60mg; Vit D 0IU; Calcium 267mg; Iron 3mg

Herby Avocado Toast with Egg or Smoked Salmon

AVOCADO TOAST IS A DELICIOUS way to start the day and can offer plenty of variety. With these few simple flavor additions, you can elevate your avocado toast game to a whole new level! If you want to switch it up during the week, you can also try avocado toast with smoked salmon for a boost of omega-3 fatty acids and even more protein.

Makes 1 serving

Ingredients:

- 1 small Hass avocado
- ⅛ teaspoon cumin
- ⅛ teaspoon smoked paprika
- ⅛ teaspoon salt
- 1 teaspoon lime juice
- 1 piece whole-wheat toast or corn tortilla
- 1 egg (hardboiled or fried) or 2 oz. smoked salmon
- Oil for pan

Directions:

1. Heat oil on medium-high heat, then fry egg until egg whites are cooked through. Or, if making smoked salmon variety, slice 2 ounces and set aside for topping.
2. In a bowl, mash 1 small avocado with ⅛ teaspoon cumin, ⅛ teaspoon smoked paprika, ⅛ teaspoon salt, and 1 teaspoon lime juice.
3. Toast bread for a crunchier taste.
4. Spread the avocado mixture onto the whole-wheat toast, place fried egg or smoked salmon on top, and enjoy!

Recipe with Fried Egg
Per serving: Kcal 384; Carb 28g; Pro 13g; Fat 26g; Sat. Fat 5g; Fiber 12g; Omega-3 0.3g; Sodium 606mg; Potassium 854mg; Magnesium 73mg; Vit D 36IU; Calcium 103mg; Iron 3mg

Recipe with Smoked Salmon
Per serving: Kcal 387; Carb 28g; Pro 18g; Fat 25g; Sat. Fat 4g; Fiber 12g; Omega-3 0.5g; Sodium 796mg; Potassium 893mg; Magnesium 78mg; Vit D 388IU; Calcium 850mg; Iron 2mg

Banana Bread Pancakes

This recipe doesn't even need butter or syrup and you can eat it like bread on the go – just like banana bread! It is one of our favorites because it offers versatility and never disappoints on flavor. Choose to make mini-pancakes, large pancakes, or put the batter in a waffle maker for added texture and excitement.

Makes ~15 mini-pancakes (analysis based on 1 mini-pancake)

Ingredients:

- 2 cups oat flour
- 4 teaspoons baking power
- ¼ teaspoon salt
- 2 eggs
- 3 medium bananas, mashed (fresh or defrost a frozen banana)
- 1¾ cups low-fat milk (or your choice of milk)
- ¼ cup canola oil
- 1 teaspoon vanilla extract
- ⅓ cup crushed or whole California walnuts (mix in batter or use as toppings)
- ⅓ teaspoon cinnamon
- *Serve with*: 2 tablespoons maple syrup (pour in a small dish and dip your pancakes)

Directions:

1. Mix all dry ingredients in a bowl.
2. Mix all wet ingredients in a separate bowl.
3. Mash a banana on a plate, then mix it into the wet ingredients.
4. Pour wet ingredients into dry ingredients and whisk until bubbly.
5. Lightly oil skillet if not using a non-stick variety, and heat skillet on medium-high heat.
6. Spoon small or large amounts of batter onto the skillet (depending on desired pancake size) or put the batter into a waffle maker.
7. Flip the pancakes when the top side and edges start to bubble.
8. Continue to cook until both sides are golden-brown and cooked through, then enjoy!

Pancakes
Per serving: Kcal 138; Carb 16g; Pro 4g; Fat 7g; Sat. Fat 1g; Fiber 2g; Omega-3 0.6g; Sodium 61mg; Potassium 179mg; Magnesium 62mg; Vit D 64IU; Calcium 208mg; Iron 1mg

2 Tablespoons maple syrup
Kcal 104; Carb 27g; Pro 0g; Fat 0g; Sat. Fat 0g; Fiber 0g; Omega-3 0g; Sodium 5mg; Potassium 85mg; Magnesium 8mg; Vit D 0IU; Calcium 41mg; Iron 0mg

Pineapple Carrot Muffins

Makes 18 large muffins (analysis based on 1 muffin)

Ingredients:
- 1¼ cups all-purpose flour
- ¾ cup whole-wheat flour
- 2 teaspoons baking powder
- ½ teaspoon baking soda
- ½ teaspoon salt
- ½ cup + 2 teaspoons vegetable oil
- ¾ cup agave nectar
- 2 eggs
- 2 teaspoons vanilla extract
- 2 (8-ounce) cans crushed pineapple, drained well (or about 1¼ cup)
- 2 cups carrot, shredded
- ½ cup walnuts

Directions:
1. Preheat oven to 350°F.
2. In a large bowl, combine the flours, baking powder, baking soda, and salt.
3. In a separate bowl, combine the oil and agave using a whisk or an electric beater.
4. Add the eggs to the oil agave mixture and whisk to combine. Add the vanilla, pineapple, carrots, and walnuts and stir until incorporated.
5. Gently stir the dry ingredients into the wet ingredients and mix until just combined, making sure not to over mix.
6. In a regular-sized muffin tin pan, place cupcake liners into the compartments, or lightly brush with olive oil. Then pour batter into the compartments.
7. Bake for about 30 minutes, or until a toothpick comes out clean. Cool for 10 minutes and enjoy!

Per serving: Kcal 194; Carb 26g; Pro 3g; Fat 9g; Sat. Fat 1g; Fiber 1g; Omega-3 0.6g; Sodium 102mg; Potassium 78mg; Magnesium 35mg; Vit D 4IU; Calcium 77mg; Iron 1mg

Cozy Apple Carrot Streusel Muffin Cups

Makes 8 muffins (analysis based on 1 muffin)

Ingredients:

- 1½ cups old-fashioned rolled oats
- ⅓ cup ground flax meal
- ½ small apple, shredded
- ½ medium carrot, grated
- 1 egg
- 2 tablespoons honey (or maple syrup)
- 1⅓ cups plain, unsweetened almond milk (or your choice of milk)
- 1 teaspoon vanilla
- 2 teaspoons cinnamon
- ¼ teaspoon nutmeg
- 1 teaspoon baking powder
- ¼ cup dried cranberries, plus more for topping
- ¼ cup pecans, chopped, plus more for topping
- 1 cup plain low-fat Greek yogurt, for topping only

Directions:

1. Preheat oven to 350°F.
2. In a muffin tin pan, lightly brush compartments with coconut oil or butter, or use non-stick liners.
3. Combine all ingredients (except the yogurt) in a large mixing bowl and spoon evenly into muffin tins, filling each cup to the top.
4. Bake for 20-25 minutes, until muffins spring back when touched and are lightly browned on top.
5. Let cool, then top each muffin with a couple spoons of yogurt.
6. Sprinkle with a few cranberries and pecans and serve.

Per serving: Kcal 179; Carb 23g; Pro 7g; Fat 7g; Sat. Fat 1g; Fiber 4g; Omega-3 1.1g; Sodium 54mg; Potassium 219mg; Magnesium 69mg; Vit D 23IU; Calcium 230mg; Iron 1mg

Mango & Raspberry Yogurt Smoothie Bowl

This bowl is naturally sweet from the tasty mix of fruits and a touch of honey. Try it for breakfast or keep it in mind for a healthy dessert at the end of the day!

Makes 2 servings

Ingredients:
- 2 cups frozen mango, chopped
- ½ cup plain nonfat Greek yogurt
- ½ cup low-fat milk (or your milk of choice)
- ½ tablespoon honey
- ½ cup raspberries
- 2 tablespoons toasted almond slices
- ⅛ teaspoon cinnamon

Add-ons: 1 cup of Cheerios

Directions:
1. In a blender, add mango, yogurt, milk and honey. Blend well until smooth.
2. Add smoothie mixture into a bowl and top off with raspberries.
3. Sprinkle the almond slices and healthy cereal on top.
4. Enjoy for a breakfast or as a refreshing dessert!

Per serving: Kcal 245; Carb 47g; Pro 9g; Fat 4g; Sat. Fat 0g; Fiber 6g; Omega-3 0g; Sodium 48mg; Potassium 263mg; Magnesium 35mg; Vit D 29IU; Calcium 190mg; Iron 2mg

Eggy Muffin Sandwiches

BATCH COOK THESE DELICIOUS EGG muffin sandwiches and then wrap them in wax paper and freeze them for another time! When you're ready to eat, pop them in the microwave for 2 minutes for a delicious and quick on-the-go breakfast. Switch things up and try these with any vegetables you'd like.

Makes 8 egg sandwiches (analysis based on 1 egg sandwich)

Ingredients:
- 8 large eggs
- 8 whole grain English muffins
- 12 tablespoons shredded low-fat mozzarella (or other cheese)
- ½ cup chopped green onion
- ½ cup chopped basil
- 1 cup chopped spinach
- 1 cup chopped broccoli
- 1 cup sliced mushrooms
- 1 tablespoon olive oil
- Salt and pepper to taste

Add-on: 3 egg whites

Directions:
1. Preheat oven to 350°F.
2. Crack the eggs into a bowl. Then add 2 tablespoons water, green onions, and basil.
3. Season with salt and pepper and whisk.
4. In a muffin tin pan, lightly brush compartments with olive oil or line with cupcake liners.
5. Add your choice of chopped vegetables to the bottom of the muffin tin and top them off with the whisked egg mixture, filling the compartment ¾ full.
6. Top with shredded cheese and place it in the oven for 12-15 minutes or until eggs are fully cooked.
7. Toast English muffins and place each egg muffin between the English muffin halves to create a sandwich.

Egg Muffin
Per serving: Kcal 117; Carb 2g; Pro 10g; Fat 8g; Sat. Fat 3g; Fiber 0g; Omega-3 0.1g; Sodium 190mg; Potassium 135mg; Magnesium 11mg; Vit D 41IU; Calcium 111mg; Iron 1mg

1 whole grain English muffin
Kcal 150; Carb 27g; Pro 6g; Fat 2g; Sat. Fat 0g; Fiber 4g; Omega-3 0g; Sodium 250mg; Potassium 0mg; Magnesium 0mg; Vit D 0IU; Calcium 60mg; Iron 1.5mg

Herbalicious Cauliflower Egg Cups

MUFFIN OR SILICON PAN RECIPES are so easy that we're back for more! This is another twist on the previous egg muffins with some added spices for a phytonutrient boost. It also has a different mix of veggies and herbs so you can make sure you're getting a variety of color and flavor in your diet.

Makes 12 muffin cups (analysis based on 1 muffin cup)

Ingredients:
- 1 (16-ounce) bag riced cauliflower (about 4½ cups) – or make your own with the directions below
- 7 eggs
- 3 cups Monterey Jack cheese (or lite Mexican cheese or cheddar cheese)
- 3 cloves garlic
- 3 tablespoons fresh chives, minced
- ½ teaspoon pepper
- ⅛ teaspoon salt
- ⅛ teaspoon smoked paprika

Directions:
1. Preheat oven to 375°F.
2. Lightly coat a muffin tin with oil.
3. If you're not using pre-made riced cauliflower, here's how to make it yourself. In a large bowl add 2 teaspoons water with the cauliflower, and seal with a silicone cover. Microwave cauliflower on high for 3 minutes, until tender.
4. Let cool for 5 minutes.
5. Scoop cauliflower into a cheesecloth, thick paper towels, or a thin, clean dishtowel and squeeze out as much liquid as possible. You can also use a fine mesh strainer and press with your hands. Once you have the cauliflower as dry as you can get it, place the florets into a food processor. Blend until the size of rice.
6. Place the riced cauliflower into a bowl and add all remaining ingredients. Stir until combined.
7. Scoop out the mixture evenly into the muffin tin and bake for 13-14 minutes or until the muffins are golden brown on top and the eggs are set.
8. Let cool and enjoy!

Per serving: Kcal 153; Carb 3g; Pro 11g; Fat 11g; Sat. Fat 6g; Fiber 1g; Omega-3 0.1g; Sodium 237mg; Potassium 178mg; Magnesium 17mg; Vit D 27IU; Calcium 236mg; Iron 1mg

Amaranth Breakfast Porridge

THIS DELICIOUS AND NUTRITIOUS TWIST on breakfast porridge is the perfect way to start your day! Amaranth is a super grain that's packed with high biological value protein, vitamins, minerals, and fiber, and, to top it all off, its unique nutty flavor is also delightful!

Makes 2 servings

Ingredients:
- ½ cup amaranth
- 1¼ cups water
- ⅓ cup unsweetened soy milk
- ½ pear
- 2 tablespoons chopped almonds

Add-ons: ½ medium banana, 1 tablespoon chia seeds

Directions:
1. Place amaranth and water in a pot and bring to a boil.
2. Leaving the lid partially on, reduce the heat to a simmer, and cook for 25-30 minutes, stirring occasionally.
3. Once all the water has been incorporated, gradually add in soy milk, until you reach the desired consistency. Your finished porridge will be slightly gelatinous.
4. To serve, pour into a bowl, top with your favorite porridge toppings, and enjoy!

The topping ideas keep going!
- If you're looking for something sweet: Try a mix of chopped pears, pecans, cinnamon and honey, or top with plain Greek yogurt, fresh fruit, and chopped nuts.
- For a fall twist: Top with a few tablespoons of pumpkin puree (look for unsweetened), honey or maple syrup, cinnamon, and walnuts.
- To make it savory: Add a fried egg, fresh chives, and black pepper.

Per serving: Kcal 251; Carb 37g; Pro 10g; Fat 8g; Sat. Fat 1g; Fiber 5g; Omega-3 0g; Sodium 10mg; Potassium 245mg; Magnesium 121mg; Vit D 0IU; Calcium 104mg; Iron 4mg

Turmeric Egg Scramble

Makes 2 servings

Ingredients:
- ½ cup chopped scallions
- ½ teaspoon turmeric
- ½ teaspoon paprika
- 4 large eggs, whisked
- 1 teaspoon olive oil
- ½ cup black beans
- ½ cup fresh red peppers, diced
- 2 tablespoons cilantro (or chopped micro cilantro or microgreens)

Add-ons: Serve with toast or a tortilla

Directions:
1. Use a nonstick skillet, or preheat olive oil in the pan on medium heat.
2. Add the turmeric and paprika and toast for 30 seconds.
3. Add scallions, black beans, and red peppers and cook for 3 more minutes.
4. Whisk eggs and combine everything until eggs are cooked.
5. Turn the heat down to medium-low heat. Eggs should be cooked slowly to maximize fluffiness.
6. Season with salt and pepper and finish with fresh cilantro.
7. Serve with whole grain bread for some quality carbohydrates, fiber, and phytonutrients.

Per serving: Kcal 242; Carb 16g; Pro 17g; Fat 12g; Sat. Fat 4g; Fiber 5g; Omega-3 0.2g; Sodium 241mg; Potassium 467mg; Magnesium 54mg; Vit D 82IU; Calcium 91mg; Iron 4mg

Creamy Dreamy Green Smoothie

(Recipe 1)

THERE ARE SOME DAYS WHEN our exercise routines make our stomachs growl and we can't seem to eat enough! This is a perfect time to opt for Recipe 2 of this combo so that you're adding some additional carbohydrates to either fuel or recover from exercise.

Makes 2 servings (use the second serving for smoothie bowl)

Smoothie Ingredients:
- 1 ripe green pear with skin
- 2 golden kiwis
- 1 cup frozen mango
- ¼ cup frozen spinach
- 1 cup orange juice
- ⅛ cup roasted, unsalted cashews (more for a creamier texture)
- 8-10 ice cubes

Smoothie Directions:
1. Combine all ingredients except the ice and mix well.
2. Once fully incorporated, add 8-10 ice cubes and blend well.
3. Enjoy your smoothie now and place the leftovers from the blender back in the refrigerator for tomorrow – keep in the blender to cut down on cleaning time now. You can then try it as Recipe 2 the following day to switch things up.

Per serving: Kcal 222; Carb 45g; Pro 5g; Fat 5g; Sat. Fat 1.5g; Fiber 3g; Omega-3 0.1g; Sodium 20mg; Potassium 631mg; Magnesium 61mg; Vit D 0IU; Calcium 72mg; Iron 1.5mg

Creamy Dreamy Green Smoothie Bowl

(Recipe 2)

THIS RECIPE TAKES THE LEFTOVERS from your smoothie yesterday and revives it with a little extra crunch and some added energy!

Smoothie Bowl Ingredients:
- Leftover serving from Recipe 1
- ⅔ cup Cheerios (add more for additional carbohydrate)
- 10 cashews (~1½ tablespoons)
- 3-5 ice cubes

Smoothie Bowl Directions:
1. Add ice to leftover smoothie and blend again.
2. Pour in bowl.
3. Top with whole grain cereal that contains less than 6 grams of sugar per serving.
4. Add in roasted unsalted cashews and enjoy.

Serve with the Turmeric Egg Scramble for added protein!

Per serving: Kcal 347; Carb 67g; Pro 6g; Fat 8g; Sat. Fat 1g; Fiber 8g; Omega-3 0g; Sodium 74mg; Potassium 742mg; Magnesium 60mg; Vit D 13IU; Calcium 128mg; Iron 7mg

Clementine French Toast

Makes 1 serving

Ingredients:

French Toast
- ½ teaspoon olive oil to coat the pan (or canola oil)
- 1 egg
- ¼ cup low-fat milk (or your choice of milk)
- 2 slices whole grain bread

Toppings:
- 2-3 tablespoons plain low-fat Greek yogurt (or flavored)
- 1 teaspoon cinnamon
- Zest from clementine
- ½ teaspoon honey (or maple syrup)
- ⅛ teaspoon vanilla or almond extract
- 2 fresh clementines

Directions:

1. In a wide, shallow bowl, whisk together the egg and choice of milk.
2. One at a time, soak each piece of bread until well saturated, making sure both sides are fully coated.
3. Grill your soaked bread in a skillet coated with olive oil over medium heat for 2-3 minutes.
4. Flip and cook for another 2-3 minutes until both sides are a lovely, golden brown.
5. Prepare Greek yogurt topping by combining all ingredients in a small bowl and mix well.
6. Spread the Greek yogurt mix over your cooked French toast, then top with fresh clementines and extra honey or syrup, if desired, and enjoy!

Per serving: Kcal 401; Carb 58g; Pro 22g; Fat 10g; Sat. Fat 3g; Fiber 8g; Omega-3 0.2g; Sodium 431mg; Potassium 669mg; Magnesium 87mg; Vit D 65IU; Calcium 330mg; Iron 3mg

Cocoa Berry Yogurt Bowl

Makes 2 servings

Ingredients:
- 2 cups frozen berries (like blueberries and raspberries)
- 4 teaspoons unsweetened cocoa powder
- 3 teaspoons chia seeds
- 10 walnut halves (or other unsalted nuts)
- 2 cups plain nonfat Greek yogurt
- Cinnamon to taste

Add-ons: 1 teaspoon honey, 1 teaspoon vanilla extract

Directions:
1. Heat frozen berries in the microwave for 60-90 seconds.
2. Mix honey, cinnamon, and vanilla extract into warm berries.
3. Add yogurt into the bowl, then mix in cocoa.
4. Top with nuts and chia seeds.

Per serving: Kcal 294; Carb 30g; Pro 27g; Fat 10g; Sat. Fat 1g; Fiber 9g; Omega-3 0.9g; Sodium 103mg; Potassium 285mg; Magnesium 16mg; Vit D 0IU; Calcium 321mg; Iron 1mg

Pear Protein Pancakes

Makes 8 servings of medium-sized pancakes (analysis based on 1 pancake)

Ingredients:
- 2 cups oat flour
- 4 teaspoons baking powder
- ¼ teaspoon salt
- ⅓ teaspoon cinnamon
- ⅛ teaspoon nutmeg
- 2 eggs
- 4 halves canned pears, mashed
- ½ cup 2% cottage cheese
- ½ cup unsweetened soy milk
- ¼ cup canola oil
- 1 teaspoon vanilla extract

Directions:
1. Combine the flour, baking powder, cinnamon, salt, and nutmeg in a large bowl and stir.
2. In a separate bowl, mash the pears with a fork to create small lumps and chunks.
3. Add the cottage cheese, eggs, milk or milk substitute, oil, and vanilla. Stir well to combine.
4. Add the wet ingredients to the bowl containing the flour mixture and whisk well to fully incorporate the ingredients.
5. To prepare the pancakes, lightly oil a griddle, cast iron skillet, or other heavy-bottomed pan and heat over medium-high heat.
6. Reduce the heat to medium-low, add about ⅓ cup of batter per pancake, and cook until bubbles form over the surface of the batter.
7. Flip the pancake and cook 30 seconds to 1 minute on the other side, or until both sides of the pancake are dark golden brown.

Per serving: Kcal 200; Carb 20g; Pro 7g; Fat 11g; Sat. Fat 1g; Fiber 3g; Omega-3 0.7g; Sodium 134mg; Potassium 132mg; Magnesium 95mg; Vit D 9IU; Calcium 341mg; Iron 2mg

Ginger Beet Smoothie

This tart and tangy smoothie is the perfect post-exercise snack and is loaded with antioxidants and nutrients. Beets are an excellent option to pair with your exercise, as some studies show that consuming beets in a certain quantity may help enhance exercise performance, improve blood flow to your brain, and decrease blood pressure. All of this is due to the natural nitrates in the beets. Plus, they are packed with betalains, a phytochemical that is a natural antioxidant. Tart cherry and pomegranate juice may also help improve exercise recovery, making this an even more powerful smoothie option. Add a little turmeric for some extra anti-inflammatory action, and your choice of protein powder for a protein boost. How's that for a power-packed smoothie?

Makes 1 serving

Ingredients:
- 2 small beets (you can save time by buying precooked beets)
- 1 cup tart cherry juice (or ½ cup tart cherry juice + ½ cup pomegranate juice)
- ¾ cup frozen blueberries
- 1 frozen medium banana
- ½ teaspoon fresh ginger
- 2 teaspoons lime juice
- ¼ cup skim milk (or your choice of milk)
- 2 tablespoons unsweetened whey protein powder (or pea protein powder)
- 1 teaspoon turmeric

Add-ons: 2 tablespoons cashews, 1-2 tablespoons agave or honey

Per serving: Kcal 461; Carb 94g; Pro 20g; Fat 3g; Sat. Fat 1g; Fiber 9g; Omega-3 0.1g; Sodium 163mg; Potassium 1134mg; Magnesium 79mg; Vit D 29IU; Calcium 196mg; Iron 4mg

Directions:
1. Combine all ingredients in a blender, add your choice of optional additions, blend well, then enjoy!

LUNCH AND DINNER

Simple Miso Soup

DOUBLE, TRIPLE OR QUADRUPLE THIS recipe to make leftovers (or some to share). Experiment with different textures of tofu and different types of miso paste to see which ones you like best. For a carbohydrate boost, add in some cooked soba noodles or serve with a side of your favorite whole grain. Brown rice and quinoa are both tasty options.

Makes 1 serving

Ingredients:
- 1½ tablespoons miso paste
- 1¾ cups water
- ¾ cup tofu, diced
- 1 tablespoon olive oil
- ¼ cup mushrooms (or carrots)
- ¼ cup zucchini
- 1 teaspoon minced garlic and/or ginger root
- 3 seaweed snack sheets, crumbled, or other dried seaweed of choice
- *Garnish*: chives, bean sprouts, sesame seeds, toasted sesame oil, or red chili flakes

Directions:
1. If opting for soba noodles or a side of grain, prepare based on the package directions.
2. Dice your vegetables and combine with tofu and olive oil in a skillet. Heat over medium heat, stirring occasionally. Once veggies are fully cooked, add the minced garlic and ginger and cook for an additional 2 minutes.
3. While your veggie and tofu mix is cooking, bring water to a boil in a medium saucepan.
4. Once water reaches a boil, pour approximately ½ cup of the water into your soup bowl with the miso paste, and dissolve by whisking with a fork.
5. Transfer the vegetable and tofu blend into your miso bowl and pour in the remaining hot water.
6. Add in any additional garnishes and enjoy!

Per serving without garnishes:
Kcal 306; Carb 8g; Pro 22g; Fat 23g; Sat. Fat 3g; Fiber 4g; Omega-3 0.6g; Sodium 1294mg; Potassium 641mg; Magnesium 82mg; Vit D 1IU; Calcium 217mg; Iron 2mg

Herbed Mushroom Barley Soup

This herbed mushroom barley soup makes for a great lunch or dinner and is vegan, if you opt not to add the egg. However, including the egg will increase the protein content and add a little heartiness to the dish. Feel free experiment and swap out barley for another whole grain.

Makes 3-4 servings (analysis based on 4 servings)

Ingredients:
- 4 cups vegetable broth (or water)
- 2 leeks, slivered (or 1 medium white or yellow onion, diced)
- 2½ cups chopped mushrooms (any kind works – you can try just one type, or use a variety)
- 3 medium carrots, diced
- 1 clove garlic, minced
- 2 tablespoons chives, chopped
- ½ teaspoon dried rosemary
- ½ teaspoon dried thyme
- 5-6 kale leaves, de-stemmed and sliced
- 1½ tablespoons olive oil
- Salt and pepper to taste

For each individual serving, add:
- ½ cup barley, precooked
- 1 fried egg

Directions:
1. Heat liquid in a medium pot.
2. While water is heating, slice leeks (or dice onion) and cook on medium heat in a large skillet lightly coated with olive oil.
3. As the leeks begin to turn golden, add the mushrooms and carrots. Add a little more oil if needed and cook for 5 more minutes.
4. Transfer vegetables to the pot with boiling water, add the garlic, most of the chives, rosemary and thyme, and cover.
5. Let simmer for about 10 minutes, adding in kale at the 8-minute mark.
6. Pour into a bowl, add ½ cup of precooked barley, and if desired, top with a fried egg.
7. Add salt and pepper to taste, and garnish with the remaining fresh chives.

Per serving: Kcal 277; Carb 38g; Pro 11g; Fat 10g; Sat. Fat 2g; Fiber 6g; Omega-3 0.2g; Sodium 953mg; Potassium 592mg; Magnesium 52mg; Vit D 39IU; Calcium 102mg; Iron 4mg

Colorful High-Protein Pasta Salad

ADD EXTRA PROTEIN TO YOUR pasta dishes by replacing regular pasta with legume pasta. Grocery stores now carry various brands of pasta made from black beans, red lentils, chickpeas, and more. They increase the protein in your meals and are naturally colorful and full of hearty fiber.

This recipe uses red lentil pasta, but you can use any legume pasta. The lentil and garbanzo bean pastas seem to be a better hit with most people than black bean. Cook until your pasta is al dente. Experiment with different types and brands to find your favorite flavor and texture. You'll save on meal costs as well because you'll have a protein punch without the addition of any animal proteins.

Makes 3-4 small servings (analysis based on 4 servings)

Ingredients:
- 4 cups arugula
- 1 cup sliced cucumber
- 12 cherry tomatoes, halved
- 1 diced medium Hass avocado
- 1 cup white kidney beans, canned (or dry that have been cooked and cooled)
- 2 cups red lentil pasta, cooked and cooled
- 3 tablespoons olive oil
- 5 tablespoons balsamic vinegar
- ½ teaspoon black pepper

Add-ons: Sprinkle of cheese, vegan cheese, or nutritional yeast

Directions:
1. In a large bowl, add arugula, cucumber, tomatoes, avocado, beans, and pasta.
2. Add olive oil, balsamic vinegar, and black pepper (or dressing of choice).
3. Using a large spoon, gently mix everything together until the dressing evenly coats all the ingredients.
4. Place in the refrigerator to cool or serve immediately.

Per serving: Kcal 312; Carb 32g; Pro 10g; Fat 16g; Sat. Fat 2g; Fiber 8g; Omega-3 0.1g; Sodium 193mg; Potassium 511mg; Magnesium 22mg; Vit D 0IU; Calcium 131mg; Iron 3mg

Chickpea Avocado Salad with Crispy Polenta Croutons

Makes 2 servings of Salad

Makes 3 servings of Polenta Croutons (save a serving for a side to Ranchero Tofu Scramble or Turmeric Egg Scramble)

Ingredients:
- 1 (15-ounce) can chickpeas/ garbanzo beans
- 1 medium Hass avocado, chopped
- 1 teaspoon olive oil
- 1 teaspoon lemon juice
- 4 cups arugula (or other leafy greens)
- Ground pepper and salt to taste

Polenta Croutons Ingredients:
- 18 ounces precooked polenta
- 2 tablespoons olive oil
- 1 teaspoon ground pepper
- 1 teaspoon garlic powder
- 1 teaspoon Italian seasoning
- 2 tablespoons parmesan cheese (or nutritional yeast)

Directions:
1. Drain and rinse the canned beans.
2. Combine the first 6 ingredients in a large bowl.
3. Cut precooked, cooled polenta into cubes and brush with olive oil and favorite seasonings to taste.
4. Bake at 350°F for 10 minutes or until crispy.
5. Add bean mixture and crunchy croutons atop a bed of greens and enjoy!

Avocado Chickpea Salad
Per serving: Kcal 331; Carb 36g; Pro 13g; Fat 17g; Sat. Fat 2g; Fiber 15g; Omega-3 0.2g; Sodium 728mg; Potassium 803mg; Magnesium 96mg; Vit D 0IU; Calcium 148mg; Iron 4mg

Polenta Croutons *(this can vary based on brand and density of corn meal)*
Per serving: Kcal 259; Carb 36g; Pro 4g; Fat 11g; Sat. Fat 2g; Fiber 2g; Omega-3 0g; Sodium 439mg; Potassium 103mg; Magnesium 20mg; Vit D 1IU; Calcium 43mg; Iron 2mg

Mediterranean Poached Egg on Toast

Makes 2 servings

Ingredients:
- ⅔ cup cannellini beans, canned, unsalted
- ½ tablespoon shallot, chopped finely
- 2 teaspoons white vinegar, plus 1 tablespoon for poaching eggs
- 1 teaspoon olive oil
- 1 small whole grain baguette
- 2 eggs
- 3 leaves fresh basil, thinly sliced
- *Garnish:* Red pepper flakes, garlic powder, salt and pepper to taste

Directions:
1. In a small bowl combine beans, shallot, vinegar, olive oil, and spices.
2. Lightly mash the beans, then set aside while you prepare the poached egg.
3. In a medium saucepan, simmer water with 1 tablespoon of white vinegar until small bubbles begin to form.
4. Gently drop in the eggs and let them cook for 4-5 minutes. Using a slotted spoon, scoop out the eggs and lay them carefully on a paper towel to remove excess water. It can be tricky at first, but you'll be a poached egg master in no time!
5. Toast slices of whole grain bread. Spread white bean mixture onto toast, and top with poached egg, fresh basil, and salt and pepper.

Per serving: Kcal 246; Carb 30g; Pro 14g; Fat 8g; Sat. Fat 2g; Fiber 6g; Omega-3 0g; Sodium 320mg; Potassium 252mg; Magnesium 47mg; Vit D 36IU; Calcium 65mg; Iron 3mg

Curried Chickpeas

Makes 6 servings

Ingredients:

- 3 (15-ounce) cans of chickpeas, drained
- 1½ cups onion, chopped
- ¾ cup tomatoes, chopped
- 3 cloves garlic, minced
- 2 tablespoons grated ginger
- 1 teaspoon cayenne pepper
- ¾ teaspoon turmeric
- ¼ cup plain whole fat Greek yogurt
- 3 tablespoons olive oil
- ¼ cup chopped cilantro
- ¾ teaspoon salt

Directions:

1. In a pot heat the olive oil on medium-low heat.
2. Add chopped onions and let them sauté for 5 minutes. Add garlic and ginger and cook for another 2 minutes.
3. Add tomatoes, cayenne pepper, salt, and turmeric. Cook for 7 minutes until mixture looks like a tomato puree.
4. Add chickpeas and yogurt and lower heat to medium-low. Let chickpeas cook for 20 minutes.
5. Finish the chickpeas with chopped cilantro.
6. Serve with a whole grain like quinoa or barley.

Per serving: Kcal 283; Carb 35g; Pro 12g; Fat 12g; Sat. Fat 2g; Fiber 11g; Omega-3 0.1g; Sodium 839mg; Potassium 462mg; Magnesium 67mg; Vit D 0IU; Calcium 101mg; Iron 3mg

Salsa Autentica Cilantro Tostada

This tostada is a plant-protein packed meal that can be enjoyed any time of day. For a vegan option, substitute the optional ingredients for your favorite vegan substitutes!

Makes 2 servings

Ingredients:

- 1 (15-ounce) can black beans, drained and rinsed
- ⅛ teaspoon cumin
- ⅛ teaspoon chili
- ⅛ teaspoon garlic powder
- 1 cup sprouted tofu
- ¼ cup of your favorite salsa
- ¼ cup cilantro
- 2 tablespoons salsa autentica
- 2 tablespoons shallot or red onion
- 2 cloves garlic, chopped
- 1 teaspoon olive oil
- *Serve with:* 2 corn tortillas

Add-ons: Spritz of lime or chili lime seasoning, 2 tablespoons lite Mexican cheese, vegan cheddar, 2 tablespoons light sour cream, or Greek yogurt

Taco Mix
Per serving: Kcal 334; Carb 40g; Pro 23g; Fat 10g; Sat. Fat 1g; Fiber 12g; Omega-3 0g; Sodium 224mg; Potassium 459mg; Magnesium 92mg; Vit D 83IU; Calcium 303mg; Iron 4mg

Two 4.5" corn tortillas
Kcal 67; Carb 13g; Pro 1g; Fat 1g; Sat. Fat 0g; Fiber 2g; Omega-3 0g; Sodium 7mg; Potassium 0mg; Magnesium 0mg; Vit D 0IU; Calcium 0mg; Iron 0mg

Directions:

1. In a bowl mix beans, your favorite salsa, and dried and fresh spices and let sit.
2. In a pan add 1 teaspoon oil and cook garlic and shallots for 3 minutes and cook over medium-high heat, then add cubed tofu and 1-2 tablespoons of salsa autentica.
3. Cook for 5 more minutes.
4. Add beans mixture and cook for 3 more minutes.
5. Serve on lightly toasted corn tortillas and eat with a knife and fork tostada style.

Chile Lime Tempeh Tacos

This recipe makes a great lunch or dinner or can even serve as a savory breakfast! Feel free to experiment with other vegetables or add in some beans or grains such as brown rice or quinoa. Multiply the ingredients if you want to make some to share. Some tempeh is a soybean and grain mix that includes barley so keep this in mind if you're looking for a gluten-free dish.

Makes 2 servings

Ingredients:
- 4 ounces tempeh, sliced
- ½ lime, juiced
- ½ medium Hass avocado, sliced
- 2 kale leaves, thinly sliced or handful of spinach
- ¼ cup zucchini, diced
- 2 teaspoons olive oil
- 1 teaspoon smoked paprika
- Salt to taste
- *Serve with:* 2 corn tortillas

Add-ons: Salsa or fresh cilantro to taste

Directions:
1. Cut tempeh into thin slices.
2. Lay the cut pieces of tempeh in a shallow dish with the lime juice and let sit for 5 minutes. While tempeh is marinating, slice the kale and zucchini.
3. Heat the olive oil in a skillet over medium heat, then add the diced zucchini and tempeh, stirring occasionally.
4. When zucchini is nearly cooked, add kale and cook several more minutes.
5. Warm the tortillas, then distribute the stir fry mix evenly between the two tortillas.
6. Top with sliced avocado, smoked paprika, and any other toppings of choice.

Tempeh Taco
Per serving: Kcal 161; Carb 6g; Pro 13g; Fat 11g; Sat. Fat 2g; Fiber 2g; Omega-3 0g; Sodium 130mg; Potassium 348mg; Magnesium 55mg; Vit D 0IU; Calcium 82mg; Iron 2mg

Two 4.5" corn tortillas
Kcal 67; Carb 13g; Pro 1g; Fat 1g; Sat. Fat 0g; Fiber 2g; Omega-3 0g; Sodium 7mg; Potassium 0mg; Magnesium 0mg; Vit D 0IU; Calcium 0mg; Iron 0mg

Black Bean, Corn, and Quinoa Salad

Makes 4 servings

Ingredients:
- 1½ cups dry quinoa
- 3 cups water
- 1 (15-ounce) can black beans, drained and rinsed
- 1 (14-ounce) jar Trader Joe's Corn and Chile Tomato-Less Salsa (or your favorite salsa)

Directions:
1. Rinse quinoa in a flour sifter or small mesh colander. Rinsing eliminates the bitter residue.
2. Cook in a pot or rice cooker with ratio of 1½ cups quinoa to 3 cups water or veggie broth.
3. Drain 1 can black beans. If you're concerned about sodium, rinse with cold water to reduce the sodium content.
4. Place 1 jar corn salsa in a bowl with black beans and quinoa. Mix together, eat, and enjoy.

Per serving: Kcal 459; Carb 87g; Pro 18g; Fat 4g; Sat. Fat 0g; Fiber 13g; Omega-3 0.2g; Sodium 646mg; Potassium 359mg; Magnesium 126mg; Vit D 0IU; Calcium 64mg; Iron 4mg

Very Veggie Sandwich

This sandwich is bursting with colorful veggies. It's my favorite lunch to pack for those busy days with a larger appetite. Put on your creative hat and experiment with other vegetable combinations too! Mixing and matching sautéed vegetables (such as mushrooms, zucchini, spinach, chard, or onion), with fresh greens (such as arugula, sprouts, or mixed salad greens) can give even more of a flavor burst.

Makes 1 serving

Ingredients:
- 2 slices 100% whole grain bread
- ~4 thin slices of eggplant
- ½ medium Hass avocado, slivered
- 1 Roma tomato, sliced
- 3 leaves kale, destemmed
- 1 tablespoon hummus
- 1 egg, fried
- 1 tablespoon olive oil
- Black pepper to taste

Directions:
1. Heat oil in a skillet over medium-low heat. Once oil is hot, add sliced eggplant and cover with a lid. Flip eggplant after 3-4 minutes.
2. While eggplant is cooking, wash and slice your other veggies.
3. Spread a layer of hummus on one slice of bread, then add the sliced avocado, black pepper, and tomato.
4. Once eggplant is nearly cooked, remove the lid and cook for another 3-4 minutes. Then add to your sandwich.
5. Fry the egg and sauté kale until just cooked. Layer these onto the sandwich, slice into halves, and enjoy!

Per serving: Kcal 590; Carb 59g; Pro 21g; Fat 33g; Sat. Fat 6g; Fiber 19g; Omega-3 0.4g; Sodium 595mg; Potassium 1480mg; Magnesium 143mg; Vit D 36IU; Calcium 211mg; Iron 4mg

Quick and Easy Farmer's Bowl

THIS BEAN AND VEGGIE BOWL can be versatile with different dressings or seasonings and is quick to prepare. Use a combination of different beans or give lentils a try. You can swap the kale for another dark leafy green, such as rainbow chard or spinach. Feel free to add in any other veggies of choice. A few of my favorites are eggplant, zucchini, and onions.

Makes 1 serving

Ingredients:
- 5-6 cremini or white mushrooms
- ½ (15-ounce) can kidney beans (or your choice of beans)
- 4 leaves kale, destemmed
- ½ medium Hass avocado, sliced
- 1½ tablespoons salsa
- 1 tablespoon olive oil
- *Serve with:* 2 corn tortillas

Adds-on: cumin, balsamic vinegar, Bragg liquid aminos, hot sauce

Directions:
1. Drain and rinse beans and combine with salsa in a medium saucepan on medium-low heat, stirring occasionally.
2. Rinse and thinly slice mushrooms. Sauté in a skillet over medium heat with the olive oil. Cover with lid to shorten cook time.
3. Rinse kale and break into bite-sized pieces. Add to skillet when mushrooms are almost fully cooked. Cook about 2 more minutes.
4. Heat corn tortillas over an open flame or in the oven until soft.
5. Combine the beans and veggies into a bowl, top with sliced avocado, and serve with the tortillas on the side. Enjoy!

Farmer's Bowl
Per serving: Kcal 447; Carb 43g; Pro 15g; Fat 26g; Sat. Fat 4g; Fiber 15g; Omega-3 0.4g; Sodium 819mg; Potassium 1366mg; Magnesium 90mg; Vit D 0IU; Calcium 125mg; Iron 3.5mg

Two 4.5" corn tortillas
Kcal 67; Carb 13g; Pro 1g; Fat 1g; Sat. Fat 0g; Fiber 2g; Omega-3 0g; Sodium 7mg; Potassium 0mg; Magnesium 0mg; Vit D 0IU; Calcium 0mg; Iron 0mg

Jackfruit Tacos

Makes 2-3 servings (analysis based on 3 servings)

Ingredients:
- 1 (9.9-ounce) can jackfruit, drained
- ½ cup salsa of choice
- 1 (15-ounce) can black beans, drained
- 2 cups chopped tri-color bell peppers
- ½ cup shredded cabbage
- 1 teaspoon paprika
- 1 teaspoon cumin
- 3 cloves garlic
- 1 tablespoon olive oil
- 1 teaspoon vegan Worcestershire sauce (purchase GF)
- Salt, black pepper, and cayenne to taste
- *Serve with:* 2 corn tortillas

Directions:
1. Rinse and drain jackfruit.
2. Add to large sauté pan with garlic, paprika, cumin, Worcestershire sauce, and olive oil on medium heat.
3. Cook for 40 minutes and add a couple of splashes water, vegetable broth, or salsa if the jackfruit starts sticking.
4. Add half the salsa and all the bell peppers. Cook another 7-10 minutes.
5. Rinse and drain the black beans, then stir into the mix in the last 2 minutes.
6. Top with additional salsa and shredded red cabbage.
7. Serve in tortillas or over rice or leafy greens.

Jackfruit Taco Mix
Per serving: Kcal 273; Carb 50g; Pro 9g; Fat 5g; Sat. Fat 1g; Fiber 10g; Omega-3 0.1g; Sodium 493mg; Potassium 722mg; Magnesium 82mg; Vit D 0IU; Calcium 100mg; Iron 3mg

Two 4.5" corn tortillas
Kcal 67; Carb 13g; Pro 1g; Fat 1g; Sat. Fat 0g; Fiber 2g; Omega-3 0g; Sodium 7mg; Potassium 0mg; Magnesium 0mg; Vit D 0IU; Calcium 0mg; Iron 0mg

Miso Chopped Salad

This bowl is packed with color, which means it offers a punch of phytochemicals. Add cooked brown rice for an extra boost of carbohydrates for hard training days.

Makes 1 serving

Ingredients:
- 1 cup chopped veggie mix (red cabbage, peppers, radishes, broccoli)
- 1 cup chopped roasted sweet potato and turnip cubes
- 1 small head baby bok choy
- 2 scallions, thinly sliced
- ½ cup cooked chickpeas (or ½ cup canned, drained)
- 1 teaspoon sesame oil
- ½ teaspoon ground ginger
- ½ teaspoon garlic powder

Dressing Ingredients:
- 1 teaspoon sesame oil
- ½ lime, juiced
- 1 tablespoon miso
- ½ teaspoon ground ginger
- 1 scallion, white part only
- ½ cup cashews
- ¼ cup water, plus a little more to thin to reach desired consistency
- Asian hot chili sauce to taste

Directions:
1. If you don't have premade sweet potatoes or turnips, chop both into quarters. Mix with a drizzle of oil and cook on a baking sheet at 350°F for 30 minutes or until tender when pierced with a fork.
2. Cut bok choy into 2-inch pieces and lightly sauté for ~7-10 minutes with 1 teaspoon sesame oil, ½ teaspoon ginger, and ½ teaspoon garlic powder.
3. Add cooked bok choy, chickpeas, chopped veggies, sweet potatoes, and turnips to a large bowl.
4. Make dressing by combining all ingredients in a food processor or blender.
5. Pour the desired dressing amount over your salad and serve.
6. Store remaining dressing in a jar in the fridge for up to 2 weeks.

Salad without Dressing
Per serving: Kcal 429; Carb 74g; Pro 14g; Fat 11g; Sat. Fat 1g; Fiber 16g; Omega-3 0.1g; Sodium 548mg; Potassium 1117mg; Magnesium 64mg; Vit D 0IU; Calcium 260mg; Iron 6mg

Full Dressing Recipe
Kcal 403; Carb 23g; Pro 12g; Fat 30g; Sat. Fat 5g; Fiber 3g; Omega-3 0.1g; Sodium 652mg; Potassium 79mg; Magnesium 12mg; Vit D 0IU; Calcium 57mg; Iron 4mg

Winter Salad

THIS SALAD TASTES GREAT ANY time of year, so if delicata squash isn't in season, opt for sweet potato or another squash instead. The light balsamic dressing balances the flavors well, but feel free to substitute it with your favorite dressing too.

Makes 1 serving

Ingredients:

- 2 cups mixed greens
- ½ small delicata squash, sliced
- ¾ cup cauliflower florets
- 2 small cooked beets, canned or vacuum packed (or steam and peel them yourself)
- ½ cup white beans, canned, drained and rinsed
- 1 tablespoon hemp seeds

Add-ons: Sprinkle of Spicy Squash Seeds (see recipe) or other seeds

Balsamic Dressing Ingredients:

- 2 tablespoons balsamic vinegar
- 4 tablespoons olive oil
- 1 teaspoon mustard seed
- 1 teaspoon honey (or agave)
- 1 teaspoon fresh parsley, finely chopped

Directions:

1. Preheat oven to 400°F.
2. Roast squash and cauliflower with a drizzle of olive oil for 35 minutes.
3. Make dressing by combining all ingredients in a small bowl or jar, mix well, and let sit for at least five minutes before mixing into salad.
4. Add lettuce, beets, roasted squash, roasted cauliflower, beans, and hemp seeds to a large plate or bowl.
5. Add dressing and mix together.
6. If desired, top with Spicy Squash Seeds (from snacks section), other nut or seed of choice, or avocado slices.

Salad without Dressing
Per serving: Kcal 358; Carb 64g; Pro 19g; Fat 6g; Sat. Fat 1g; Fiber 15g; Omega-3 1.3g; Sodium 802mg; Potassium 2255mg; Magnesium 222mg; Vit D 0IU; Calcium 233mg; Iron 8mg

Full Dressing Recipe
Kcal 545; Carb 12g; Pro 1g; Fat 57g; Sat. Fat 8g; Fiber 0g; Omega-3 0g; Sodium 9mg; Potassium 43mg; Magnesium 4mg; Vit D 0IU; Calcium 22mg; Iron 2mg

Kale Super Salad Bowl

WHEN BUILDING A SALAD FOR your main meal, load it up with grains, protein, and healthy fats, alongside all of the colorful veggies. This way, you'll feel full and fueled until it's time for your next meal. This delicious kale salad recipe is one you can always fall back on for a simple plant-based salad that won't disappoint.

Makes 1 bowl

Ingredients:
- 3-4 kale leaves
- 1 carrot, sliced thin
- ¼ medium cucumber, sliced thin
- 1 hard-boiled egg
- ½ medium Hass avocado, chopped
- ½ cup brown rice (or quinoa)
- ½ teaspoon olive oil

Add-ons: ⅓ cup white beans, Bragg liquid aminos, balsamic vinegar

Lemon-Tahini Dressing Ingredients:
- Juice from ½ lemon
- 1 tablespoon chopped chives
- 1 tablespoon olive oil
- ½ teaspoon minced garlic
- Dash of salt and pepper

Directions:
1. Mix the dressing ingredients together in a large mug or jar.
2. Slice or rip the kale into bite-sized pieces, then massage with a drizzle of olive oil for 1-2 minutes on a hard surface.
3. Thinly slice the carrot and cucumber and cut the avocado into bite-sized pieces.
4. In a medium bowl, combine the kale with the remaining salad ingredients, add dressing, and mix well.

Salad with Dressing
Per serving: Kcal 486; Carb 43g; Pro 13g; Fat 32g; Sat. Fat 5g; Fiber 10g; Omega-3 0.3g; Sodium 559mg; Potassium 939mg; Magnesium 93mg; Vit D 38IU; Calcium 117mg; Iron 2mg

Middle-Eastern Eggplant Pita

This cauliflower eggplant pita dish is inspired by Israeli cuisine and is loaded with tasty flavors and tons of veggies. It makes the perfect healthy lunch or dinner. For a protein boost, add your choice of tofu, beans, or chicken. *Tip: Bake extra cauliflower and eggplant to have as leftovers for meals later in the week!*

Makes 1 serving

Ingredients:
- 1 pita bread
- ½ cup diced cauliflower
- ½ cup diced eggplant
- 1 tablespoon olive oil
- 1 teaspoon paprika
- 1 teaspoon cumin
- ½ Roma tomato, diced
- 2 scallions, thinly sliced

Add-ons: 3 ounces baked skinless chicken, 6 ounces baked tofu, ½ small Hass avocado, 2 ounces crumbled feta cheese

Tahini Sauce Ingredients:
- 2 tablespoons tahini
- 2 tablespoons plain low-fat Greek yogurt
- 1 clove garlic, finely chopped
- 2 sprigs parsley, minced
- ½ tablespoon fresh lemon juice
- 2 tablespoons hot water
- Salt and pepper to taste

Directions:
1. In a bowl or jar, combine all of the tahini sauce ingredients and mix well.
2. Dice eggplant and cauliflower, coat with olive oil, paprika, and cumin, and bake in the oven at 350°F for about 30 minutes or until tender, stirring occasionally.
3. Dice Roma tomato and thinly slice scallions. Prepare any optional toppings of choice.
4. Once veggies are finished baking, remove from oven and warm your pita bread. Slice off the top third and place the smaller third into the bottom of the larger piece- this will help reinforce your pita pocket.
5. Carefully fill your pita with roasted veggies and fresh tomato and scallions, then dress with tahini sauce and enjoy.

Per serving: Kcal 540; Carb 53g; Pro 17g; Fat 32g; Sat. Fat 5g; Fiber 7g; Omega-3 0.3g; Sodium 600mg; Potassium 797mg; Magnesium 77mg; Vit D 0IU; Calcium 209mg; Iron 6mg

Walnut Crusted Salmon with Ginger Broccoli

THIS DISH PROVIDES A HELPFUL boost of omega-3 fatty acids. Pair with a whole grain for a satisfying meal.

Makes 4 servings

Ingredients:
- 16 ounces salmon
- ¼ cup chopped parsley
- ½ cup whole-wheat panko (or GF panko)
- ½ cup chopped walnuts
- 1 tablespoon mustard
- 1 teaspoon olive oil
- 2 tablespoons minced ginger
- 1 head broccoli, cut in florets
- Salt and pepper to taste

Directions:
1. Preheat oven to 350°F.
2. In a small bowl combine parsley, whole-wheat panko, walnuts, salt, and pepper.
3. Brush salmon with mustard and then top it with the walnut mixture.
4. Place the salmon topping side up on baking sheet and bake in the oven for 15 minutes.
5. Heat olive oil over medium heat in a small sauté pan.
6. Add chopped ginger and cook for 1 minute.
7. Add broccoli and cook for 4-5 minutes making sure it is still crunchy.
8. Season with salt and pepper.
9. Serve with baked salmon.

Per serving: Kcal 435; Carb 20g; Pro 31g; Fat 27g; Sat. Fat 5g; Fiber 6g; Omega-3 4.4g; Sodium 293mg; Potassium 998mg; Magnesium 91mg; Vit D 500IU; Calcium 105mg; Iron 3mg

Roasted Beet, Goat Cheese, and Spinach Salad

ADD A NUTRIENT BOOST TO your day with this spinach and beet salad—it's so simple to prepare, yet absolutely delicious and loaded with vitamins, minerals, and phytochemicals. The creaminess of goat cheese is a lovely complement to the texture of roasted beets. Two homemade dressing options are included here—try them both and see which one you like best. Opting for the Classic Balsamic Herb Dressing will also help boost your daily herb intake, which may lead to added health benefits. Herbs have a variety of powerful properties, including antimicrobial, anti-inflammatory, and antioxidant functions.

Makes 2 servings

Ingredients:
- 2 medium beets
- 1 teaspoon olive oil
- 3 cups baby spinach leaves
- 4 tablespoons crumbled goat cheese

Add-ons: Diced apple, red onion, or cucumber for some extra crunch and added flavor; quinoa, whole grain toast, barley

Two Choices for Dressing:

Honey Mustard Dressing:
- 1 tablespoon Dijon mustard
- 1 tablespoon apple cider vinegar
- 1 tablespoon olive oil
- ⅓ teaspoon honey
- Salt and pepper to taste

OR

Classic Balsamic Herb Dressing:
- 2 tablespoons olive oil
- 2 tablespoons balsamic vinegar
- ¾ teaspoon honey
- 1½ teaspoons of your choice of dried Italian herbs (such as oregano, basil, rosemary and thyme)
- Salt and pepper to taste

Directions:
1. Preheat oven to 400°F.
2. Rub peeled beets with olive oil, then wrap in aluminum foil. Roast for about one hour, or until tender. To speed up cook time, pre-cut beets into smaller pieces prior to roasting.
3. While the beets are roasting, prepare your dressing of choice by combining all ingredients into a large mug or jar, then whisking together well.
4. Once beets have finished baking, let cool, then slice into wedges.
5. Assemble your salad by laying baby spinach, crumbled goat cheese, and beets into a bowl or plate. Add any optional toppings of choice.
6. Drizzle with dressing, then enjoy!

Salad without Dressing
Per serving: Kcal 103; Carb 9g; Pro 5g; Fat 6g; Sat. Fat 3g; Fiber 4g; Omega-3 0g; Sodium 156mg; Potassium 267mg; Magnesium 19mg; Vit D 0IU; Calcium 46mg; Iron 2mg

Honey Mustard Dressing Full Recipe
Kcal 142; Carb 2g; Pro 0g; Fat 14g; Sat. Fat 2g; Fiber 0g; Omega-3 0.1g; Sodium 480mg; Potassium 14mg; Magnesium 0mg; Vit D 0IU; Calcium 1mg; Iron 0mg

Classic Balsamic Herb Dressing Full Recipe
Kcal 284; Carb 10g; Pro 0g; Fat 27g; Sat. Fat 4g; Fiber 0g; Omega-3 0.2g; Sodium 248mg; Potassium 43mg; Magnesium 4mg; Vit D 0IU; Calcium 11mg; Iron 0mg

Melissa's Sloppy Joes

THIS SPIN ON YOUR CLASSIC sloppy joes might sound strange, but it is an undeniable hit with anyone who tries them! The flavor and texture will still meet your expectations while offering a huge boost in nutritional value. Soy the star ingredient of this recipe, has been shown to lower risk of heart disease and is loaded with phytochemicals that can help protect against cancer.

Makes 3 servings

Ingredients:
- 6 ounces tofu
- 14 ounces fresh or canned drained diced tomatoes
- 2 tablespoons tomato paste
- ½ cup sweet onion, chopped
- 2 garlic cloves, finely chopped
- ¼ cup chopped bell pepper
- 1 cup cooked lentils
- ½ teaspoon smoked paprika
- 1 tablespoon corn starch
- ½ teaspoon cumin
- 1 teaspoon chili powder
- 2 teaspoons dry mustard powder
- 2 teaspoons soy sauce
- 3 whole-wheat hamburger buns

Directions:
1. Rinse and drain the tofu, then crumble it into small bits using a fork.
2. In a pan over medium heat, sauté onions and garlic.
3. In another pan, add tofu and chili powder and mix until combined.
4. Cook on medium-high heat for 4-5 minutes, mixing occasionally.
5. Add in the sautéed onions and garlic with the lentils and cook for 5-7 minutes.
6. Add in the remaining ingredients and simmer on low heat for 30 minutes.
7. In a small bowl mix cornstarch with 2 tablespoons of water, then mix into the rest of the pan.
8. Enjoy on whole-wheat hamburger buns with salad and homemade chips or fries.

Sloppy Joes Mix
Per serving: Kcal 210; Carb 32g; Pro 14g; Fat 4g; Sat. Fat 0g; Fiber 10g; Omega-3 0.1g; Sodium 735mg; Potassium 747mg; Magnesium 39mg; Vit D 0IU; Calcium 184mg; Iron 4mg

1 whole-wheat hamburger bun
Kcal 151; Carb 25g; Pro 7g; Fat 2g; Sat. Fat 1g; Fiber 3g; Omega-3 0.1g; Sodium 239mg; Potassium 136mg; Magnesium 45mg; Vit D 0IU; Calcium 111mg; Iron 1mg

Hearty Sloppy Joes

FOR THOSE OF YOU WHO can't quite get past the idea of no meat in your sloppy joes, here is a mix to 'meat' you half way (no pun intended!).

Makes 3 servings

Ingredients:
- 3 ounces tofu
- 3 ounces ground turkey (or chicken)
- 14 ounces fresh or canned drained diced tomatoes
- 2 tablespoons tomato paste
- ½ cup sweet onion, chopped
- 2 garlic cloves, finely chopped
- ¼ cup bell pepper, chopped
- ½ cup white beans, cooked
- ½ teaspoon smoked paprika
- 1 tablespoon corn starch
- ½ teaspoon cumin
- 1 teaspoon chili powder
- 2 teaspoons dry mustard powder
- 2 teaspoons soy sauce
- 1 teaspoon Worcestershire sauce
- 3 whole-wheat buns

Directions:
1. Rinse and drain the tofu, then crumble it into small bits using a fork. Mash white beans with a fork.
2. In a medium pan, sauté onions and garlic.
3. In another pan, add tofu, meat, Worcestershire sauce, and chili powder and mix until combined.
4. Cook on medium-high heat for 4-5 minutes, mixing occasionally until meat is fully browned.
5. Add sautéed onions, garlic, and lentils and cook for 5-7 minutes.
6. Add remaining ingredients and simmer on low heat for 30 minutes.
7. In a small bowl mix the corn starch with 2 tablespoons of water, then mix into the pan.
8. Enjoy on whole-wheat hamburger buns with salad and homemade chips or fries.

Sloppy Joes Mix
Per serving: Kcal 213; Carb 27g; Pro 16g; Fat 5g; Sat. Fat 1g; Fiber 7g; Omega-3 0.1g; Sodium 976mg; Potassium 778mg; Magnesium 44mg; Vit D 2IU; Calcium 157mg; Iron 4mg

1 whole-wheat hamburger bun
Kcal 151; Carb 25g; Pro 7g; Fat 2g; Sat. Fat 1g; Fiber 3g; Omega-3 0.1g; Sodium 737mg; Potassium 136mg; Magnesium 45mg; Vit D 0IU; Calcium 111mg; Iron 1mg

TVP Chicken Burgers

LOOKING TO CUT YOUR BEEF and sugar intake? This burger subs some of your chicken with textured vegetable protein (TVP) for a simple boost of plant-based protein. To cut down on sugar, use ½ ketchup and ½ tomato sauce for the ketchup ingredient. Caramelized onions taste great, but roasted peppers can too – be creative with your plant-based foods!

Makes 2 burgers (analysis based on 1 burger)

Ingredients:
- 1 cup chopped baby portabella mushrooms
- ¼ cup TVP + ¼ cup warm water
- 6 ounces ground chicken
- 1 tablespoon soy sauce
- 1 tablespoon balsamic vinegar
- 1 teaspoon dried thyme
- 1 minced garlic clove
- 1 large beefsteak tomato (for toppings)
- ¾ cup arugula
- 1 large half-sour pickle
- *Serve with*: whole-wheat hamburger bun

Add-ons: ¼ large (or ½ small) Hass avocado, 1 tablespoon ketchup, 2 tablespoons caramelized onions, salt and pepper to taste

Directions:
1. Reconstitute TVP with water and let sit 5-10 min.
2. Over medium heat, cook mushrooms with garlic, thyme, soy sauce, and balsamic vinegar, until most of the liquid is absorbed or about 10 minutes.
3. Add mushrooms, TVP, and ground meat to a food processor. Pulse until combined.
4. Mold into burgers and wet hands in between if it gets too sticky.
5. Cook on medium heat until cooked thoroughly (3-5 min each side, depending on thickness). You can also choose to broil or barbeque them.
6. Build your burger with a hamburger bun, tomato, arugula, pickle, and add any of the additional toppings of choice.

TVP Chicken Burger
Per serving: Kcal 269; Carb 21g; Pro 33g; Fat 10g; Sat. Fat 2g; Fiber 5g; Omega-3 0.2g; Sodium 1223mg; Potassium 486mg; Magnesium 38mg; Vit D 11IU; Calcium 94mg; Iron 4mg

1 whole-wheat hamburger bun
Kcal 151; Carb 25g; Pro 7g; Fat 2g; Sat. Fat 1g; Fiber 3g; Omega-3 0.1g; Sodium 239mg; Potassium 136mg; Magnesium 45mg; Vit D 0IU; Calcium 111mg; Iron 1mg

Umami Black Bean Beet Burgers

LOAD THESE BURGERS WITH TOMATOES, lettuce, pickles and your toppings of choice. Serve with a side of jicama for a refreshing crunch and a variety of phytochemicals.

Makes 8 burgers (analysis based on 1 burger)

Ingredients:
- ½ cup brown rice, cooked
- 1 cup mushrooms, finely chopped
- 1 tablespoon gluten-free soy sauce
- 2 teaspoons balsamic vinegar
- 2 garlic cloves, minced
- ⅓ red onion, finely diced
- 1 tablespoon olive oil + oil for grill pan
- 1 (15-ounce) can black beans, drained and rinsed
- 1 cup steamed beets, finely grated
- 1 tablespoon parsley, chopped
- Pinch of salt
- Pinch of black pepper
- 1 teaspoon cumin
- ½ teaspoon chili lime powder
- ¼ teaspoon smoked paprika
- 3 tablespoons egg, beaten
- ⅓ cup oat flour
- *Serve with:* whole-wheat or GF hamburger buns

Directions:
1. In a mixing bowl, mix black beans, beets, parsley, and seasonings together, and lightly mash the black beans.
2. Add the mushroom mixture into the bowl and mix well.
3. Add the egg and oat flour and check the consistency. Add more egg if mixture is too dry or more flour if mixture is too sticky or moist.
4. Form the mixture into patties and place on a grill or sauté pan. Cook for 3-4 minutes on each side.
5. Put the patties on burger buns and add toppings of choice.

Burger
Per serving: Kcal 139; Carb 22g; Pro 7g; Fat 3g; Sat. Fat 1g; Fiber 6g; Omega-3 0.1g; Sodium 320mg; Potassium 325mg; Magnesium 50mg; Vit D 19IU; Calcium 29mg; Iron 2mg

1 whole-wheat hamburger bun
Kcal 151; Carb 25g; Pro 7g; Fat 2g; Sat. Fat 1g; Fiber 3g; Omega-3 0.1g; Sodium 239mg; Potassium 136mg; Magnesium 45mg; Vit D 0IU; Calcium 111mg; Iron 1mg

Stuffed Pepper with Brown Lentil Salad

Makes 2 servings

Ingredients:
- 1 red bell pepper, halved
- 1 cup cooked brown lentils
- 2 radishes, thinly sliced
- 2 tablespoons green onions, chopped
- 1 tablespoon cilantro, chopped
- 2 tablespoons olive oil
- 2 lemons, juiced
- Salt and pepper to taste

Add-ons: Balsamic vinegar, Bragg liquid aminos, feta

Directions:
1. Heat oven to 350°F.
2. Place bell pepper halves on coated baking sheet or silicon baking mat and roast for 15 minutes.
3. Cook brown lentils according to package instructions, then allow them to cool.
4. In a medium bowl, add lentils, radishes, green onions, cilantro, olive oil, lemon juice, salt, and pepper.
5. Stuff the slightly cooled peppers with the lentil salad.

Per serving: Kcal 257; Carb 25g; Pro 9g; Fat 14g; Sat. Fat 2g; Fiber 9g; Omega-3 0.2g; Sodium 316mg; Potassium 540mg; Magnesium 44mg; Vit D 0IU; Calcium 32mg; Iron 4mg

Gallo Pinto Rice

This Gallo Pinto is a traditional breakfast dish from Costa Rica, but the savory flare fits more closely with our typical lunch or dinner flavors. Traditionally, it is served with eggs and sour cream, but you can serve it with nonfat sour cream or nonfat plain Greek yogurt for a healthier alternative.

Makes 2 servings

Ingredients:
- 1 cup uncooked brown rice
- 1 tablespoon olive oil
- 1 cup black beans with liquid from cooking, do not drain
- ¼ cup cilantro
- ½ cup red, orange, or green bell peppers (or multiple colors), finely chopped
- ¼ cup sweet onion, finely chopped
- 1 tablespoon Salsa Lizano (if Salsa Lizano is not available, substitute with GF Worcestershire sauce)*
- Salt to taste

Directions:
1. Prepare the rice according to cooking instructions. Cook rice with a little less water if you prefer an al dente texture.
2. Prepare the beans according to cooking instructions.
3. In a skillet, heat oil on medium heat.
4. Add the onion, bell pepper, and cook until onions are translucent.
5. Add the rice, black beans with liquid, and Worchester sauce. Turn the heat to medium-low and simmer about 8-10 minutes or until water is absorbed. Stir occasionally.
6. Mix in cilantro and salt to taste.
7. Enjoy with a dollop of plain, nonfat Greek yogurt.

*Worcestershire sauce used for analysis

Per serving: Kcal 561; Carb 103g; Pro 16g; Fat 10g; Sat. Fat 2g; Fiber 12g; Omega-3 0.2g; Sodium 401mg; Potassium 814mg; Magnesium 210mg; Vit D 0IU; Calcium 84mg; Iron 4mg

Marinara Zoodles

MAKE EXTRA ZUCCHINI NOODLES AND store in the back of your refrigerator for up to 4 days.

Makes 6-8 servings (analysis based on 6 servings)

Ingredients:
- 2 teaspoons olive oil
- 3 cloves garlic, minced
- 4 medium zucchinis, spiralized into noodles
- 24 ounces low-sodium marinara sauce
- ½ cup shredded parmesan cheese or nutritional yeast
- Salt and pepper to taste
- *Garnish:* fresh basil

Add ons: beans, chicken, side of toast with hummus

Directions:
1. In a medium skillet over medium heat, warm the oil. Add the garlic and sauté for 2-3 minutes, until fragrant.
2. Add zucchini noodles and cook 3-4 minutes, until noodles are just starting to get tender. Season with salt and pepper to taste.
3. Add marinara sauce, cheese, and fresh basil to each serving.

Per serving: Kcal 123; Carb 14g; Pro 6g; Fat 5g; Sat. Fat 2g; Fiber 3g; Omega-3 0.2g; Sodium 238mg; Potassium 716mg; Magnesium 48mg; Vit D 1IU; Calcium 138mg; Iron 1mg

Red Lentil Mac 'n' Cheese

THERE IS SOMETHING COMFORTING ABOUT sitting down to a warm bowl of macaroni and cheese, yet the traditional recipe is generally low in the vegetable, protein, and fiber department. This recipe adds a few unique twists to up the nutrient density without sacrificing taste. With red lentils blended into the cheese sauce, your choice of either gluten-free or whole grain pasta, and a bit of green veggies mixed in, you can enjoy this bowl of cheesy deliciousness AND get an extra nutrient punch! Made with chickpea flour, it packs in 14 grams of protein per serving and is also an excellent source of fiber and iron. Be careful not to overcook to avoid soggy noodles.

Makes 4 servings

Ingredients:

- 2 cups cooked red lentils (or yellow split peas)
- 1 cup low-fat milk
- 2 tablespoons olive oil
- 2 tablespoons whole-wheat flour, or almond flour for gluten-free version (or other gluten-free flour)
- 1½ cups low-fat shredded cheddar cheese
- ¼ teaspoon fresh garlic powder (or fresh garlic)
- 1 cup broccoli florets (or green peas)
- 1 pound cooked whole-wheat or gluten-free pasta (we used Banza)
- Salt and pepper to taste

Add-ons: Dash of cumin, chili powder or paprika

Directions:

1. Cook lentils according to package instructions.
2. Once lentils are fully cooked, puree them along with the milk in a food processor or blender.
3. In a small saucepan heat the olive oil over medium heat, then slowly add flour, whisking continually.
4. Next, whisk in the blended red lentil and milk mixture, then stir in cheese, garlic, salt, pepper, and optional chili powder for an added kick.
5. Steam or blanch your green veggie of choice and cook the pasta according to package instructions.
6. Mix everything together, then enjoy!

Mac and Cheese
Per serving: Kcal 484; Carb 66g; Pro 29g; Fat 13g; Sat. Fat 4g; Fiber 9g; Omega-3 0.2g; Sodium 529mg; Potassium 559mg; Magnesium 107mg; Vit D 31IU; Calcium 296mg; Iron 5mg

Mac and Cheese (gluten-free)
Per serving: Kcal 525; Carb 73g; Pro 27g; Fat 14g; Sat. Fat 4g; Fiber 7g; Omega-3 0.2g; Sodium 530mg; Potassium 464mg; Magnesium 53mg; Vit D 31IU; Calcium 289mg; Iron 4mg

Mahi Mahi Fish Tacos

These fish tacos may seem intimidating, but frozen fish in vacuumed seal bags just require scissors, a baking pan, and an oven timer. Make sure to use corn tacos for a gluten-free option.

Makes 4 servings

Mahi Mahi Ingredients:
- 2 tablespoons olive oil
- 1½ pounds (24 ounces) fresh mahi mahi fish
- ½ cup shredded lite Mexican cheese

Coleslaw Ingredients:
- 2½ cups green cabbage, shredded
- 1 teaspoon white balsamic vinegar or white rice vinegar
- ⅛ teaspoon cayenne (red pepper)
- ⅛ teaspoon smoked paprika
- ⅛ cup yellow mustard
- 1½ teaspoons honey
- ⅓ cup reduced-fat mayonnaise

Pico de Gallo Ingredients:
- 4 medium, ripe tomatoes, diced (about 3 cups)
- 1 cup cilantro, packed (about ½ cup cilantro, chopped)
- ¼ cup red onion, minced
- ¼ teaspoon cumin
- ⅛ teaspoon salt
- 2 tablespoons fresh lime juice

Serve with: 2 corn tortillas or toasted corn tacos

Directions:
1. Preheat oven to 400°F.
2. Coat a baking dish with a touch of olive oil and place the mahi mahi inside.
3. Bake for 24 minutes, flipping halfway through, until fish is cooked throughout and you can gently flake it.
4. In a medium mixing bowl, combine all coleslaw ingredients.
5. In separate medium mixing bowl combine the Pico de Gallo ingredients.
6. Heat up the tortillas.
7. Layer the mahi mahi, coleslaw, and Pico de Gallo on each tortilla.
8. Sprinkle with cheese and serve.

Mahi Mahi
Per serving: Kcal 245; Carb 1g; Pro 35g; Fat 11g; Sat. Fat 3g; Fiber 3g; Omega-3 0.2g; Sodium 260mg; Potassium 708mg; Magnesium 51mg; Vit D 0IU; Calcium 226mg; Iron 2mg

Coleslaw
Per serving: Kcal 41; Carb 9g; Pro 1g; Fat 1g; Sat. Fat 0g; Fiber 3g; Omega-3 0g; Sodium 264mg; Potassium 1mg; Magnesium 0mg; Vit D 0IU; Calcium 13mg; Iron 0mg

Pico de Gallo
Per serving: Kcal 29; Carb 7g; Pro 1g; Fat 0g; Sat. Fat 0g; Fiber 2g; Omega-3 0g; Sodium 81mg; Potassium 336mg; Magnesium 16mg; Vit D 0IU; Calcium 19mg; Iron 0.5mg

Two 4.5" corn tortillas
Kcal 67; Carb 13g; Pro 1g; Fat 1g; Sat. Fat 0g; Fiber 2g; Omega-3 0g; Sodium 7mg; Potassium 0mg; Magnesium 0mg; Vit D 0IU; Calcium 0mg; Iron 0mg

Mushroom Sunflower Seed Burger

THESE VEGAN BURGERS HAVE A delightful meaty texture and subtle nutty flavor. Try these out the next time you're craving a veggie burger!

Makes 8 burgers (analysis based on 1 burger)

Ingredients:
- 2 tablespoons ground flax seed (or whole chia seeds)
- ¼ cup water
- 1 medium yellow onion (or white), diced
- 15 button mushrooms (or cremini), diced
- ½ cup sunflower seeds
- ½ cup rolled oats
- 2 cloves fresh garlic
- 1½ tablespoons olive oil
- 1 teaspoon dried basil
- ½ teaspoon cayenne pepper
- 8 whole grain hamburger buns or GF hamburger bun
- Salt and black pepper to taste

Directions:
1. Preheat oven to 375°F.
2. In a medium mixing bowl, combine chia seeds or ground flax with water, then set aside.
3. Mince the garlic and dice the onion and mushrooms. Then briefly pulse this mixture in a food processor or blender until the mix is finely chopped.
4. Heat a skillet with olive oil over medium heat, then sauté the garlic, onion, and mushroom mixture for about 5 minutes, or until onions caramelize. Stir occasionally.
5. While the vegetables are sautéing, blend the oats, sunflower seeds, and spices in the food processor or blender until coarsely blended.

6. Once veggies are cooked, combine all ingredients in a medium mixing bowl and stir well.

7. Form into patties, then place onto a baking sheet lined with parchment paper. Bake at 375°F for about 30-35 minutes, or until center is fully cooked. Flip patties halfway through.

8. Serve on a whole grain hamburger bun and pair with your favorite burger toppings. I love these with sliced tomato, avocado, and lettuce. Enjoy!

Burger
Per serving: Kcal 110; Carb 8g; Pro 3g; Fat 8g; Sat. Fat 1g; Fiber 2g; Omega-3 0.4g; Sodium 86mg; Potassium 240mg; Magnesium 25mg; Vit D 0IU; Calcium 23mg; Iron 1mg

1 whole-wheat hamburger bun
Kcal 151; Carb 25g; Pro 7g; Fat 2g; Sat. Fat 1g; Fiber 3g; Omega-3 0.1g; Sodium 239mg; Potassium 136mg; Magnesium 45mg; Vit D 0IU; Calcium 111mg; Iron 1mg

Red Lentil Kabocha Curry

Makes 4 servings

Ingredients:
- 2 cups red lentils, dry
- 2 cups plain unsweetened almond milk
- 1½ cups water, more as needed
- 1 kabocha squash, seeds removed
- 2 medium zucchinis
- 16 button mushrooms (or cremini)
- 1 medium yellow onion (or white), diced
- 5 leaves chard
- 1 clove garlic, diced
- 2 teaspoons fresh ginger, diced
- 1½ tablespoons olive oil
- 1 (16-ounce) container tofu, extra firm
- 1 teaspoon cumin
- 2 teaspoons curry powder
- 1 teaspoon garam masala
- Red or black pepper to taste
- *Garnish:* Fresh herbs of choice

Add-ons: Serve with whole-wheat pita bread or your favorite whole grain, and sliced avocado

Directions:
1. Preheat oven to 350°F.
2. Destem the chard, setting the leaves aside. Cut chard stems, kabocha squash, mushrooms, and zucchini into bite-sized pieces, and dice the onion.
3. Spread the cut veggies evenly onto a baking sheet, drizzle with olive oil, and bake for about 45 minutes or until veggies are tender. Stir occasionally.
4. While your vegetables are roasting, cook the lentils. In a large pot, combine lentils, water, almond milk, minced garlic and ginger, and dried spices.
5. Cover with a lid and bring to a boil, then reduce heat to a simmer. Cook for about 15 minutes or until lentils are soft, making sure to check the water and adding more as needed.
6. Cut the tofu into bite-sized cubes and sliver the chard leaves. Add these to the pot once the lentils are fully cooked.
7. When the roasted vegetables are done, add them to the pot. Stir well, then let the mixture simmer for several minutes.
8. Enjoy your curry on its own, or pair with whole grain pita bread, cooked quinoa, brown rice, or your favorite whole grain. Garnish with fresh herbs and optional sliced avocado. Enjoy!

Per serving: Kcal 645; Carb 96g; Pro 40g; Fat 14g; Sat. Fat 2g; Fiber 17g; Omega-3 0.3g; Sodium 178mg; Potassium 1344mg; Magnesium 104mg; Vit D 55IU; Calcium 589mg; Iron 12mg

Ginger Honey Tofu

THIS TOFU TASTES GREAT COLD on top of salads, but my friends and family love it best on top of brown rice served with broccolini and other veggies.

Makes 6 servings

Ingredients:

- 1½ tablespoons olive oil (or canola oil)
- 2 (16-ounce) packages pressed organic tofu*, cubed
- 3½ tablespoons finely shredded ginger (press firmly into tablespoon)
- 3½ tablespoons chopped garlic (about 12 medium garlic cloves – I clearly LOVE garlic)
- 3 tablespoons balsamic vinegar
- 4 tablespoons honey (or agave)
- 3 tablespoons Bragg liquid aminos (or soy sauce – not GF)

If you can't purchase pressed tofu, then make your own. Place tofu in between clean dish towels, then put a cutting board on top of it. Next, place something heavy on top of the cutting board, like a cast iron pan or full kettle. Let it sit for about 10-15 minutes, and the liquid will come out, creating a pressed, meatier tofu.

Directions:

1. Cut tofu into cubes.
2. Heat oil over medium-low heat, then add tofu and turn it over every couple of minutes to prevent it from sticking. The goal is to have it lightly brown.
3. While browning, shred ginger on the smallest grater option and place in bowl.
4. Peel garlic and chop, or toss into the food processor, then add it to the bowl.
5. Pour the balsamic vinegar, honey and Bragg liquid aminos into the bowl and mix all ingredients together.
6. Evenly distribute the sauce over the tofu and cook for another 2-3 minutes on low heat.

Per serving: Kcal 210; Carb 18g; Pro 15g; Fat 10g; Sat. Fat 1g; Fiber 1g; Omega-3 0g; Sodium 518mg; Potassium 51mg; Magnesium 4mg; Vit D 0IU; Calcium 285mg; Iron 2mg

Ginger Lime Quinoa Salad

Makes 2-3 servings (analysis based on 3 servings)

Ingredients:
- 3 large shiitake mushroom caps, sliced
- 1 large red bell pepper, sliced
- 12-14 Anaheim peppers (or shishito peppers)
- ⅔ cup sprouted quinoa, dry
- 1 cup edamame, shelled
- 2 garlic cloves
- 2 teaspoons freshly grated ginger
- 1½ tablespoons coconut aminos
- 2 teaspoons sesame oil
- 1½ teaspoons miso
- 1 lime, juiced

Add-ons: 1 tablespoon sliced almonds

Directions:
1. Prepare quinoa according to package.
2. Sauté garlic in sesame oil on medium heat.
3. Add peppers and cook for 7-10 minutes.
4. Add mushrooms, miso, and coconut aminos to the pan and cook for an additional 5-7 minutes.
5. Stir in cooked quinoa, edamame, ginger, and lime juice.
6. Serve hot or refrigerate overnight and serve cold.

Per serving: Kcal 342; Carb 53g; Pro 17g; Fat 8g; Sat. Fat 1g; Fiber 11g; Omega-3 0.3g; Sodium 263mg; Potassium 640mg; Magnesium 120mg; Vit D 3IU; Calcium 101mg; Iron 5mg

Farro, Black Beans, and Tofu Bowl

FARRO IS A LESS COMMONLY known whole grain. It's an ancient form of wheat that's higher in fiber, protein, antioxidants and minerals when compared to the modern form of wheat. With a nutty and subtly sweet flavor, farro makes an excellent alternative to rice or quinoa. See how you like it in this hearty, veggie and protein-loaded bowl.

Makes 6 servings

Ingredients:

- 3 cups cooked farro, cooked in water or vegetable broth
- 1 (16-ounce) package firm tofu, cut into small cubes
- 1 can black beans, drained and rinsed
- 6 button mushrooms, sliced thinly
- 2 medium zucchinis, diced
- 1½ cup cherry tomatoes, whole
- ½ yellow onion (or white), diced
- 2 cloves garlic, minced
- 2 tablespoons olive oil
- 1¾ tablespoons soy sauce (or Bragg liquid aminos)

Add-ons: Garnish with sliced chives or green onion

Directions:

1. Cook farro according to instructions on package. For extra flavor, use vegetable broth instead of water. Look for a low-sodium vegetable broth to cut back on added salt.
2. While farro is cooking, sauté the onion in olive oil over medium heat in a large skillet or wok.
3. Once onions are translucent, add the remaining vegetables and tofu. Sauté until veggies are tender.
4. Add the beans, then cook for several more minutes.
5. To serve, place farro in a bowl, top with sautéed veggie, bean, and tofu mix, and drizzle with soy sauce or liquid aminos.
6. Add optional chives or green onions for extra flavor and enjoy!

Per serving: Kcal 315; Carb 43g; Pro 19g; Fat 8g; Sat. Fat 1g; Fiber 10g; Omega-3 0g; Sodium 451mg; Potassium 604mg; Magnesium 70mg; Vit D 0IU; Calcium 202mg; Iron 3.5mg

Sweet Potato Mac 'n' Cheese

Makes 6-8 servings (analysis based on 7 servings)

Ingredients:

- 2 boxes Banza Chickpea Pasta Mac and Cheese Classic Cheddar
- 1 box Banza Chickpea Pasta Mac and Cheese Deluxe
- ½ cup low-fat milk
- 3 tablespoons butter
- 1 cup pureed sweet potato

Directions:

1. Cook pasta according to package directions and set aside.
2. In a large saucepan over medium-low heat, heat milk and butter. Add the two powdered cheese packets from the two boxes of Banza Classic Cheddar and the creamy cheese packet from the box of Banza Deluxe. Stir in sweet potato, stirring frequently, until heated thoroughly.
3. Mix in cooked pasta and serve.

Per serving: Kcal 359; Carb 43g; Pro 20g; Fat 15g; Sat. Fat 7g; Fiber 9g; Omega-3 0g; Sodium 775mg; Potassium 350mg; Magnesium 2mg; Vit D 24IU; Calcium 191mg; Iron 3mg

Curried Egg Salad on Millet Bread

Makes 2 servings

Ingredients:
- 1 tablespoon reduced-fat mayo made with olive oil
- 2½ tablespoons 2% (or nonfat) plain Greek yogurt
- 1¾ teaspoons spicy brown mustard
- 1 teaspoon curry powder
- 1 teaspoon cumin
- 1 teaspoon pepper
- 4 hard-boiled eggs
- 2 hard-boiled egg whites
- *Serve with*: 1 slice millet bread

Add-ons: 2 tablespoons caramelized onions

Directions:
1. Using an egg slicer, slice eggs, rotate 90 degrees and slice again. Don't have an egg slicer? Dice into small squares.
2. Mix together the Greek yogurt and the mayo. Add in all the spices to the yogurt mixture and stir to combine.
3. Stir yogurt and spice mixture into the eggs.
4. Serve on millet bread or any whole grain toast with vegetables.

Egg salad
Per serving: Kcal 213; Carb 4g; Pro 18g; Fat 12g; Sat. Fat 3g; Fiber 1g; Omega-3 0g; Sodium 292mg; Potassium 220mg; Magnesium 18mg; Vit D 87IU; Calcium 89mg; Iron 2mg

1 slice millet bread
Kcal 80; Carb 14g; Pro 5g; Fat 3g; Sat. Fat 0g; Fiber 3g; Omega-3 0g; Sodium 100mg; Potassium 0mg; Magnesium 0mg; Vit D 0IU; Calcium 10mg; Iron 1mg

Cumin Tacos with Ginger Broccoli

This garlic ginger broccoli is for garlic lovers!

Makes 2 servings of each

Taco Ingredients:
- 1 (15-ounce) can kidney beans, drained
- ⅛ teaspoon cumin
- ⅛ teaspoon chili
- ⅛ teaspoon garlic powder
- ¼ cup your favorite salsa
- 2 tablespoons salsa autentica
- *Serve with:* 2 toasted corn tacos

Add-ons: 2 tablespoons reduced fat shredded Jack cheese, lite Mexican cheese or vegan cheddar, nonfat sour cream or vegan sour cream

Taco Directions:
1. Mix all ingredients in a bowl and microwave for 2-3 minutes.
2. Place mixture inside two taco shells, then top with cheese.

Garlic Ginger Broccoli Ingredients:

- 1 tablespoon ginger, thinly sliced
- 6 garlic cloves, minced
- 1 bunch broccolini
- 2 tablespoons olive oil
- ⅛ teaspoon salt
- 2 teaspoons Bragg liquid aminos (or soy sauce – not gluten-free)
- 6 tablespoons water

Garlic Ginger Broccoli Directions:

1. Cut off broccoli stem 1 inch from the end.
2. Peel the ginger and slice thinly, then mince garlic..
3. Separate the stems and florets.
4. In a skillet, heat oil over medium heat.
5. Add garlic, ginger, and salt and cook until slightly golden.
6. Add the stems and 4 tablespoons water and cook for 5-8 minutes, until softer.
7. Add the florets and 2 tablespoons water and cook for another 3-5 minutes.
8. Mix with soy sauce.

Taco Mix
Per serving: Kcal 185; Carb 34g; Pro 11g; Fat 1g; Sat. Fat 0g; Fiber 12g; Omega-3 0.1g; Sodium 425mg; Potassium 569mg; Magnesium 66mg; Vit D 0IU; Calcium 64mg; Iron 3mg

2 hard shell corn tacos
Kcal 100; Carb 13g; Pro 1g; Fat 5g; Sat. Fat 2g; Fiber 1g; Omega-3 0g; Sodium 90mg; Potassium 0mg; Magnesium 0mg; Vit D 0IU; Calcium 13mg; Iron 0mg

Ginger Garlic Broccoli
Per serving: Kcal 159; Carb 6g; Pro 4g; Fat 15g; Sat. Fat 2g; Fiber 3g; Omega-3 0.1g; Sodium 486mg; Potassium 226mg; Magnesium 24mg; Vit D 0IU; Calcium 116mg; Iron 2mg

Savory Veggie Stew

This Mediterranean inspired stew is surprisingly simple and quick to prepare. It's perfect for those times when you're craving soup but are short on time. It pairs well with fresh sourdough bread.

Makes 5 servings

Ingredients:
- 1 small onion, diced
- 2 teaspoons olive oil
- 2 medium carrots, diced
- 2 garlic cloves, minced
- 1 teaspoon dried basil
- 1 teaspoon dried thyme
- 2 bay leaves
- 2 (15-ounce) cans cannellini beans, drained and rinsed
- 1 can diced tomato (look for low-sodium)
- 32 ounces vegetable broth
- 1-2 cups water
- 1 bunch kale, destemmed and thinly sliced
- Salt and pepper to taste

Directions:
1. Heat olive oil in large pot over medium heat.
2. Add onions and cook until translucent.
3. Add carrots, garlic, herbs, beans, diced tomato, vegetable broth, water, and optional tofu.
4. Cover and let simmer until carrots are tender, about 3-5 minutes.
5. Stir in kale, salt and pepper to taste, and allow the mix to simmer for 3-5 more minutes.
6. Pour the mix into soup bowls and top with parmesan if desired.

Add-ons: For a protein boost, add in 3 ounces of cubed tofu. For cheese lovers, top with freshly grated parmesan cheese or vegan cheese.

Per serving: Kcal 229; Carb 39g; Pro 12g; Fat 2g; Sat. Fat 0g; Fiber 17g; Omega-3 0g; Sodium 494mg; Potassium 325mg; Magnesium 12mg; Vit D 0IU; Calcium 213mg; Iron 3mg

Chili Bean Tacos

Makes 4 servings

Ingredients:
- 1 (15-ounce) can kidney beans, drained and rinsed (if you want to lower sodium)
- 1 (15-ounce) can organic vegetarian chili with red beans and onions
- ¼ cup chopped red onions
- ¼ cup chopped cilantro
- ½ cup chopped cherry tomatoes
- ½ teaspoon garlic powder
- ½ teaspoon cumin
- ½ teaspoon paprika
- *Serve with:* 2 toasted corn tacos

Add-ons: 2 tablespoons nonfat Greek yogurt or light sour cream or vegan sour cream, 2 tablespoons lite Mexican cheese or vegan cheese, 2 tablespoons feta, 2 tablespoons salsa, ½ chopped avocado

Directions:
1. Chop red onion and place in ice water. This removes the bitterness and brings out the sweetness.
2. Rinse the beans in a colander, place in a bowl, then add the spices.
3. Wash and chop the tomatoes and cilantro and place in a separate bowl.
4. Heat the beans for 3-4 minutes on the stove top or for 2 minutes in the microwave.
5. Lightly toast the corn tacos.
6. Drain the red onions, add them to the bean bowl with tomatoes, and mix.
7. Place the bean mixture in the tacos, garnish with desired add-ons, and enjoy!

Taco Mix
Per serving: Kcal 184; Carb 30g; Pro 12g; Fat 2g; Sat. Fat 0g; Fiber 10g; Omega-3 0.1g; Sodium 313mg; Potassium 330mg; Magnesium 35mg; Vit D 0IU; Calcium 75mg; Iron 3mg

2 hard shell corn tacos
Kcal 100; Carb 13g; Pro 1g; Fat 5g; Sat. Fat 2g; Fiber 1g; Omega-3 0g; Sodium 90mg; Potassium 0mg; Magnesium 0mg; Vit D 0IU; Calcium 13mg; Iron 0mg

Chickpea of the Sea

THIS BEAN-BASED VARIATION OF TUNA salad uses chickpeas as a base, making it a great plant-based, protein-packed alternative to this classic dish. Enjoy as a stand-alone snack, a tasty side dish, spread on your favorite whole grain bread or crackers, or place a scoop into a whole grain tortilla or lettuce leaf and roll up to make a wrap.

Makes 2 servings

Ingredients:
- 1 cup chickpeas, drained and mashed with a fork
- ¼ cup red bell pepper, diced
- ¼ cup celery, diced
- ¼ cup purple onion, diced
- 2 tablespoons chopped dill pickle
- 1 tablespoon mustard
- 1 tablespoon low-fat mayo or vegan mayo
- 1 teaspoon garlic or sprinkle of garlic powder
- ½ teaspoon paprika
- Salt and pepper to taste
- Several sprigs fresh parsley to garnish
- *Serve with*: whole-wheat toast or salad

Add-on: Splash of fresh Meyer lemon juice

Directions:
1. Mix all ingredients together in a medium bowl, put on top of bread or leafy greens, and enjoy!

Per serving: Kcal 136; Carb 21g; Pro 6g; Fat 3g; Sat. Fat 0g; Fiber 7g; Omega-3 0.1g; Sodium 1089mg; Potassium 247mg; Magnesium 37mg; Vit D 0IU; Calcium 56mg; Iron 2mg

Creamy Kale and Potato Soup

THIS VEGAN KALE AND POTATO soup is delightfully creamy and bursting with flavors from fresh herbs and lemon! Make sure to bake the potatoes ahead of time and put them in the fridge to cool before making the soup. This allows for the formation of resistant starches.

Makes 6 servings

Ingredients:

- 1 tablespoon olive oil
- ½ medium white onion, diced
- 2 garlic cloves, minced
- 3 cups low-sodium vegetable broth
- 1 cup celery, diced
- 1 teaspoon fresh thyme, chopped
- ½ teaspoon fresh oregano, chopped
- ½ teaspoon fresh parsley
- ¼ teaspoon cumin
- ¼ teaspoon garlic powder
- 1 tablespoon Meyer lemon juice
- 2 medium potatoes (or 2 cups potatoes)
- 2 cups plain unsweetened almond milk (or soy milk)
- 4 cups kale, destemmed and sliced thin
- Salt, pepper, and chili pepper to taste

Directions:

1. Wash and scrub potato well. Vent with fork. Rub skin lightly with olive oil and salt and wrap in tinfoil to retain moisture. Bake at 350°F for 60 minutes. Then cool, and chill completely in the refrigerator for a few hours or until the next day.
2. Heat the olive oil and onion in a small skillet over medium heat. Sauté for about 5 minutes or until onion begins to brown. Add the garlic and cook for another 2 minutes.
3. Pour broth into a large pot, add onion and garlic mixture, and bring to a boil.
4. Reduce heat to a simmer, then add celery, herbs, and spices, and cook for about 10-15 minutes.
5. While soup is simmering, blend potatoes and almond milk in a food processor or blender, then pour into the soup pot.
6. After 10-15 minutes of simmering, stir in the kale and remove from heat.
7. Garnish with fresh herbs and Meyer lemon juice and enjoy!

Per serving: Kcal 115; Carb 19g; Pro 3g; Fat 3g; Sat. Fat 0g; Fiber 3g; Omega-3 0g; Sodium 382mg; Potassium 428mg; Magnesium 26mg; Vit D 37IU; Calcium 224mg; Iron 1mg

Loaded Baked Potato - Two Ways

These baked potato toppings will bring your classic baked potato to a whole new level. Plus, as you just learned, cooling your potato after baking enhances its nutrition quality. The resistant starches that form have probiotic functions, can improve the health of your gut bacteria, and may play a role in strengthening your immune system. Try out each of the topping suggestions and see which one you like best!

Mexican Style

Makes 1 serving

Ingredients:

- 1 medium russet potato
- 1 teaspoon olive oil
- Dash of salt
- ½ cup kidney beans, drained, rinsed and lightly mashed
- 2 tablespoons shredded low-fat cheese or vegan cheese
- 1-2 tablespoons fresh salsa
- 1 tablespoon plain nonfat Greek yogurt or vegan sour cream
- Fresh cilantro, to garnish
- *Optional garnish: Dash of smoked paprika*

Savory Brunch Style

Makes 1 serving

Ingredients:
- 1 medium russet potato
- 1 teaspoon olive oil
- 1 fried egg
- ½ medium mashed Hass avocado
- 1-ounce kale (2-3 kale leaves), slivered and sautéed in ¼ tablespoon olive oil
- 2 teaspoons fresh dill, chopped
- 1 tablespoon fresh Meyer lemon juice
- Salt and pepper to taste

Directions:
Note: Bake your potato early to allow time for it to fully chill prior to eating.

1. Preheat oven to 325°F.
2. Rinse and scrub the potato, rub with olive oil and salt, poke once with a fork, wrap tightly in aluminum foil, and place on a baking sheet.
3. Place in oven and allow to bake for about 1½ hours or until center is tender.
4. Remove from oven, let cool, then place in the fridge to chill fully.
5. Once the potato is chilled and you're ready to enjoy, slice the potato down the center, top with your style of choice, and enjoy!

Mexican Style Potato
Per serving: Kcal 354; Carb 59g; Pro 16g; Fat 7g; Sat. Fat 1g; Fiber 10g; Omega-3 0.1g; Sodium 941mg; Potassium 1239mg; Magnesium 87mg; Vit D 1IU; Calcium 149mg; Iron 3mg

Savory Brunch Style Potato
Per serving: Kcal 465; Carb 48g; Pro 12g; Fat 27g; Sat. Fat 5g; Fiber 9g; Omega-3 0.1g; Sodium 413mg; Potassium 1319mg; Magnesium 73mg; Vit D 0IU; Calcium 81mg; Iron 3mg

Sweet Potato Nachos

Makes 4 servings

Ingredients:
- 6 medium sweet potatoes (~2 pounds)
- 2 teaspoons olive oil
- 1 teaspoon cumin
- 1 teaspoon cayenne pepper
- 1 teaspoon paprika
- ½ teaspoon pepper
- Salt to taste right before serving

Choose Toppings:

Vegetarian Toppings:
- 1⅓ cup low-fat shredded cheddar cheese
- 8 tablespoons plain nonfat Greek yogurt (or low-fat)
- 1 chopped bell pepper
- 2 small chili peppers (remove seeds)
- 4 tablespoons chives
- 2 medium Hass avocados, chopped, sprinkled with lime juice
- ⅓ cup salsa
- 2 medium tomatoes (or about 10 cherry tomatoes)
- 3 (15-ounce) cans black beans (or beans of your choice)

Or

Vegan Toppings:
- 1⅓ cup shredded vegan cheese
- 8 tablespoons vegan sour cream
- 1 chopped bell pepper
- 2 small chili peppers (remove seeds)
- 4 tablespoons chives
- 2 medium Hass avocados, chopped, sprinkled with lime juice
- ⅓ cup salsa
- 2 medium tomatoes (or about 10 cherry tomatoes)
- 3 (15-ounce) cans black beans (or beans of your choice)

Directions:
1. Preheat oven to 450°F.
2. Wash and scrub the sweet potatoes.
3. Thinly slice sweet potatoes and place in bowl.
4. Coat sweet potatoes with olive oil by lightly tossing them in a bowl with a spoon until evenly coated.
5. Sprinkle in herbs and spices and toss again.
6. Place on a coated baking sheet coated with 1 teaspoon olive oil or use a silicone mat.
7. Bake 30 minutes, flipping halfway through. Don't turn the oven off quite yet!
8. Prepare the toppings while the potatoes bake.
9. Put your selected toppings on the sweet potatoes and place back in the oven for 3 minutes until cheese melts.
10. Add chopped avocado, eat, and enjoy.

Vegetarian Recipe
Per serving: Kcal 711; Carb 108g; Pro 38g; Fat 16g; Sat. Fat 3g; Fiber 35g; Omega-3 0.1g; Sodium 829mg; Potassium 2582mg; Magnesium 87mg; Vit D 2IU; Calcium 375mg; Iron 7mg

Vegan Recipe
Per serving: Kcal 868; Carb 123g; Pro 26g; Fat 34g; Sat. Fat 13g; Fiber 37g; Omega-3 0.1g; Sodium 1128mg; Potassium 2527mg; Magnesium 81mg; Vit D 0IU; Calcium 281mg; Iron 7mg

5-Minute Microwave African Peanut Soup

USING DEHYDRATED ONIONS IN PLACE of diced fresh onions makes for a quick cooking, flavor-packed soup. Always consider the length of time that will be needed for vegetables to become tender in the microwave. Choose vegetables that cook quickly, like frozen peas, canned beans, canned stewed tomatoes, salsa, summer squash, Swiss chard, or baby kale.

Makes 1 serving

Ingredients:

- 1 tablespoon tomato paste
- ¼-inch chunk peeled ginger
- 1 garlic clove, finely minced
- ¼ cup canned pumpkin (or pumpkin puree)
- ⅛ cup all-natural peanut butter
- 1 teaspoon Bragg liquid aminos (or low-sodium soy sauce – not GF)
- 1 tablespoon dehydrated onions
- 2 cups baby greens
- 1½ cups low-sodium vegetable broth
- ¼ teaspoon salt
- ¼ - ½ teaspoon sriracha hot sauce

Add-ons: 2 tablespoons roasted peanuts, fresh cilantro for topping

Directions:

1. In a quart-sized Mason jar, combine tomato paste, ginger, garlic, pumpkin puree, peanut butter, soy sauce, dehydrated onions, baby greens, low-sodium vegetable broth, salt, and sriracha.
2. Cover with lid and shake jar vigorously.
3. Remove the lid and microwave on high for 4-5 minutes.
4. Enjoy it now, or cool to room temperature, cover with lid, and store in the refrigerator for up to 5 days.
5. When ready to serve, microwave for 3-4 minutes to reheat. Serve soup topped with roasted peanuts and fresh cilantro or pour over a bed of brown rice or quinoa.

Per serving: Kcal 381; Carb 37g; Pro 13g; Fat 16g; Sat. Fat 3g; Fiber 10g; Omega-3 0g; Sodium 1336mg; Potassium 106mg; Magnesium 6mg; Vit D 0IU; Calcium 219mg; Iron 14mg

Amaranth Veggie Soup

Makes 4-5 servings (analysis based on 4 servings)

Ingredients:
- 1 onion, minced
- 1 teaspoon olive oil
- 2 carrots, diced
- 1 bell pepper, diced
- 2 stalks celery, diced
- 2 cloves garlic, diced
- 2 cups water
- 2 cups low-sodium vegetable broth (substitute for regular sodium if you are looking to increase your sodium intake based on exercise)
- 1½ cups cooked amaranth
- Several sprigs each of fresh thyme, oregano, and parsley, minced
- Salt and pepper to taste

Directions:
1. Cook amaranth according to instructions on the package.
2. In a large saucepan, heat olive oil and onion over medium heat and cook for 5-7 minutes, until shallot becomes translucent.
3. Add vegetable broth and remaining vegetables to the pot, cover, reduce heat to a simmer, and cook until veggies are soft.
4. While soup is simmering, blend cooked amaranth with 2 cups water, then pour into the soup.
5. When veggies are tender, remove from heat, season with fresh herbs, salt, and pepper, and enjoy!

Per serving: Kcal 154; Carb 28g; Pro 5g; Fat 3g; Sat. Fat 0g; Fiber 5g; Omega-3 0g; Sodium 411mg; Potassium 290mg; Magnesium 68mg; Vit D 0IU; Calcium 99mg; Iron 3mg

SNACKS/SIDES

Wholesome Homemade Bread

THIS BREAD IS MOST DELICIOUS when enjoyed right away! You can top it with a healthy butter substitute if you're craving something savory, or add a spoonful of honey or jam for a little extra sweetness. It is also good for sandwiches or served on the side of soup.

Makes 2 loaves (1 loaf makes 14 slices) (analysis based on 1 slice)

Ingredients:
- 2 tablespoons honey
- 2½ cups warm water
- 2 packages dry active yeast
- 3 cups whole-wheat flour
- 1 cup white flour + extra for cutting board
- 1 cup oat flour
- 1 cup rolled oats
- 1½ teaspoons salt
- 2½ tablespoons coconut oil (or olive oil or margarine)

Directions:
1. Coat two bread pans generously with oil or a plant-based butter substitute.
2. In a medium bowl, dissolve the honey and yeast in warm water and set aside for about 10 minutes.
3. In a large bowl, combine the dry ingredients.
4. Combine the wet ingredients with the dry, then transfer to a clean, floured surface and knead for at least 10 minutes.
5. Place the dough into a lightly greased bowl, cover loosely with a clean cloth, and set aside in a warm place to allow it to rise for an hour.
6. Knead again for at least 10 minutes, then divide dough into two even pieces. Form them into the shape of loaves, place them in the bread pans, cover, and allow it to rise again for another hour.
7. Place the pans in oven and bake at 350°F for 30-40 minutes, or until tops are golden brown.
8. Remove from the oven, transfer to cooling rack, and lightly oil the tops.
9. For storing leftovers, cover with a cloth until fully cool, then transfer to an airtight bag.

Per serving: Kcal 99; Carb 18g; Pro 3; Fat 2g; Sat. Fat 1g; Fiber 2g; Omega-3 0g; Sodium 106mg; Potassium 77mg; Magnesium 22mg; Vit D 12IU; Calcium 8mg; Iron 1mg

Spicy Squash Seeds

THESE ARE GREAT FOR SNACKING or topping salads. They're delicious with the flavors in the Winter Salad!

Makes 4-6 servings (analysis based on 6 servings)

Ingredients:
- 1½ cups cleaned seeds from one winter squash
- 1 teaspoon smoked paprika
- ½ teaspoon turmeric
- 2 teaspoons olive oil
- Pinch of black pepper

Add-on: pinch of cayenne pepper

Directions:
1. Preheat the oven to 425°F.
2. In a large mixing bowl, combine cleaned seeds, spices, and oil.
3. Spread out on a large baking sheet.
4. Bake for ~10min at 425°F, flipping halfway through. Watch them carefully–time may vary based on dryness of seeds and oven variations.
5. Let the seeds cool completely.
6. Store in airtight container in fridge.

Per serving: Kcal 195; Carb 4g; Pro 10g; Fat 17g; Sat. Fat 3g; Fiber 2g; Omega-3 0.1g; Sodium 3mg; Potassium 275mg; Magnesium 192mg; Vit D 0IU; Calcium 16mg; Iron 3mg

Sesame Spinach Sauté

Makes 1 serving

Ingredients:
- 1 cup low-sodium vegetable broth
- 4 cups packed fresh spinach
- 1 tablespoon lime juice
- 1 teaspoon sesame oil
- Salt and pepper to taste

Directions:
1. Pour broth into a medium saucepan and bring to a boil.
2. Add spinach, then cook for 3-5 minutes or until spinach is just wilted, stirring occasionally.
3. Remove from heat and drain excess liquid. *TIP: Save extra liquid in the fridge or freezer to use as a base in soup or to make cooked grains.*
4. Add in lime juice, sesame oil, salt and pepper, and stir well.
5. Enjoy as a side dish or as a nutrient-loaded snack.

Per serving: Kcal 99; Carb 10g; Pro 4g; Fat 5g; Sat. Fat 1g; Fiber 5g; Omega-3 0g; Sodium 561mg; Potassium 21mg; Magnesium 1mg; Vit D 0IU; Calcium 184mg; Iron 6mg

Ranchy Popcorn Snack

Makes 2 servings

Ingredients:

- 6 cups cooked popcorn kernels (or 3 tablespoons uncooked kernels)
- ¼ teaspoon garlic powder
- ¼ teaspoon onion powder
- 1 tablespoon parmesan cheese, grated (or nutritional yeast)
- ½ teaspoon dried parsley flakes

Directions:

1. Heat a sauté pan on medium heat. Add popcorn kernels and shake pan continuously for 1-2 minutes. Don't worry if a few seeds won't pop. Transfer popped popcorn to a large bowl.
2. Combine the garlic powder, onion powder, parmesan cheese, and dried parsley in a small bowl.
3. Top your popcorn with a sprinkle of your home-made ranch topping. Mix well with spoon and enjoy.

Per serving: Kcal 104; Carb 20g; Pro 4g; Fat 2g; Sat. Fat 0g; Fiber 4g; Omega-3 0g; Sodium 48mg; Potassium 88mg; Magnesium 34mg; Vit D 0IU; Calcium 26mg; Iron 0mg

Mini Egg Frittata

Makes 6 mini frittatas (analysis based on 1 mini frittata)

Ingredients:
- 1 small onion, diced
- 2 cloves garlic, finely chopped
- 1 tablespoon olive oil
- 6 eggs
- 1 medium tomato, diced into small cubes
- 1 cup spinach, finely chopped
- ¼ teaspoon salt
- ¼ teaspoon pepper
- Cooking spray as needed

Directions:
1. Preheat oven to 375°F.
2. In a small pan heat olive oil on medium heat.
3. Sauté the onion and garlic until translucent, about 5 minutes.
4. Allow onions and garlic to cool.
5. In a medium bowl whisk the eggs.
6. Add the tomato, spinach, and onion/garlic sauté to the egg mixture.
7. Coat the mini-muffin tins with cooking spray. Pour egg mixture into the muffin tins.
8. Bake at 375°F until eggs are cooked through, about 18-20 minutes.
9. Let cool, then enjoy!

Per serving: Kcal 96; Carb 3g; Pro 6g; Fat 7g; Sat. Fat 2g; Fiber 1g; Omega-3 0.1g; Sodium 148mg; Potassium 155mg; Magnesium 12mg; Vit D 36IU; Calcium 36mg; Iron 1mg

"Cheesy" Greens

Makes 2-3 servings (analysis based on 2 servings)

Ingredients:
- 3 cups mixed leafy greens
- ½ tablespoon olive oil
- 2 tablespoons nutritional yeast
- 1 teaspoon turmeric
- 1 tablespoon sun-dried tomatoes
- 1 tablespoon hemp seeds

Add-ons: Pinch of black pepper, cayenne pepper, or salt

Directions:
1. Sauté the greens with oil, nutritional yeast, and spices for 5-7 minutes.
2. Top with tomatoes and hemp seeds.
3. Serve as a side dish or add ½ cup beans or an egg to round out the meal.

Per serving: Kcal 89; Carb 5g; Pro 5g; Fat 6g; Sat. Fat 1g; Fiber 3g; Omega-3 0.6g; Sodium 24mg; Potassium 364mg; Magnesium 60mg; Vit D 0IU; Calcium 35 mg; Iron 2mg

Pea Protein Energy Bars

WITH ONLY THREE INGREDIENTS, THESE energy bars are both wholesome and very simple to make. Filled with healthy fats, plant-based protein, and naturally sweetened with dates, they are perfect for in-between meals or as a pre-exercise snack!

Makes 10 bars (analysis based on 1 bar)

Ingredients:
- 1⅓ cups dates, finely chopped
- 2 cups unsalted peanuts
- ¾ cup unsweetened pea protein powder

Directions:
1. Combine all ingredients in a food processor or blender and blend well.
2. Form into bars, small cubes, or energy balls.
3. Store in an airtight container in the fridge or freezer until you're ready to enjoy.

Per serving: Kcal 259; Carb 22g; Pro 14g; Fat 15g; Sat. Fat 2g; Fiber 4g; Omega-3 0g; Sodium 86mg; Potassium 354mg; Magnesium 49mg; Vit D 0IU; Calcium 48mg; Iron 4mg

Buttery Corn

EAT THIS ON WEEKENDS AS a mid-morning snack, an afternoon pick-me-up, or as a dinner side. This simple recipe provides lutein and zeaxanthin – important phytochemicals for eye and heart health – and is unexpectedly delicious. You can also prepare carrot coins the same way!

Makes 1 serving

Ingredients:

- 1 cup frozen organic sweet corn (or roasted corn)
- 1 teaspoon olive oil
- 1 teaspoon healthy butter substitute
- Dash of salt and pepper

Directions:

1. Heat 1 cup frozen organic sweet corn or roasted corn in microwave.
2. After heating, add 1 teaspoon of olive oil, 1 teaspoon butter substitute, a dash of salt and pepper, and stir until mixed.

Per serving: Kcal 238; Carb 34g; Pro 4g; Fat 10g; Sat. Fat 2g; Fiber 2g; Omega-3 0g; Sodium 284mg; Potassium 4mg; Magnesium 0mg; Vit D 0IU; Calcium 1mg; Iron 1mg

Hummus Loaded Sweet Potato

Makes 1 serving (or batch cook several in the oven to use for 3-4 days)

Ingredients:
- 1 sweet potato (medium, around 5 inches)
- 2 tablespoons hummus
- 1½ tablespoons plain soy yogurt
- Dash of pepper

Add-ons: Herbs of choice

Directions:
1. Rinse and scrub the potato then pierce with fork to vent.
2. Microwave for 3-5 minutes. For oven-baked, wrap tightly in tinfoil for an extra tender and caramelized sweet potato. Preheat oven to 425°F and bake for 45 minutes. Check at 30 minutes as oven temperatures range.
3. Place in oven and allow to bake for about 1½ hours or until center is tender.
4. Top with hummus, soy yogurt, and any other herbs of choice (dill tastes great!).

Per serving: Kcal 185; Carb 35g; Pro 5g; Fat 3g; Sat. Fat 1g; Fiber 6g; Omega-3 0g; Sodium 194mg; Potassium 522mg; Magnesium 64mg; Vit D 0IU; Calcium 81mg; Iron 2mg

Hearty Farmer's Market Scones

These scones are loaded with veggies, contain whole grains and heart-healthy nuts and seeds, and are subtly sweet—in fact, they're sweetened only with fruit! I love eating them as an on-the-go breakfast with coffee or tea, a quick snack, or a healthy after-meal treat.

Makes 6 scones (analysis based on 1 scone)

Ingredients:

- 1 ripe medium banana
- ¾ cup apple, grated (about one small apple)
- 1 cup grated zucchini (about one medium zucchini)
- 1 cup grated carrot (about 2-3 medium carrots)
- ¼ cup raisins
- 1 teaspoon fresh grated ginger
- 1 tablespoon vegetable oil
- 1 egg, beaten
- 1 tablespoon chia seeds
- ¼ cup unsweetened almond milk
- 1½ cups whole-wheat flour
- 1 cup rolled oats
- ½ teaspoon cinnamon
- 1 teaspoon baking soda
- ⅛ teaspoon salt
- ¼ cup chopped walnuts (or your favorite types of seeds or chopped nuts)

Directions:

1. Preheat oven to 375°F.
2. Lightly oil a baking sheet.
3. In a small bowl, mix the chia seeds with the almond milk and set aside.
4. In a medium bowl, mash the banana and combine with the remaining wet ingredients.
5. In a separate bowl, combine the dry ingredients and mix well.
6. Incorporate the wet ingredients (including your chia mixture) into the dry and mix until well-combined.
7. Shape into rounded scones and place on the baking sheet. Bake for about 20 minutes, or until a toothpick inserted into the center comes out clean.
8. Remove from oven, let cool, and enjoy!

Add-ons: Dark chocolate baking chips or chunks, or protein powder

Per serving: Kcal 288; Carb 47g; Pro 9g; Fat 9g; Sat. Fat 1g; Fiber 8g; Omega-3 0.9g; Sodium 281mg; Potassium 474mg; Magnesium 84mg; Vit D 11IU; Calcium 75mg; Iron 2mg

Gluten-Free Hearty Farmer's Market Scones

Makes 6 scones (analysis based on 1 scone)

Ingredients:
- 1 ripe medium banana
- ¾ cup apple, grated (about one small apple)
- 1¼ cup raisins
- 1 teaspoon fresh grated ginger
- 1 tablespoon vegetable oil
- 1 egg, beaten
- 2 tablespoons chia seeds
- ¼ cup unsweetened almond milk
- 1½ cups almond flour
- 1 cup rolled oats
- ½ teaspoon cinnamon
- 1 teaspoon baking soda
- ⅛ teaspoon salt
- ¼ cup chopped walnuts (or other nuts or seeds)

Add-ons: Dark chocolate baking chips or chunks, or protein powder

Directions:
1. Preheat oven to 375°F.
2. Lightly oil a baking sheet.
3. In a small bowl, combine chia seeds and almond milk and set aside.
4. In a medium bowl, mash the banana and combine with the remaining wet ingredients.
5. In a separate bowl, combine the dry ingredients and mix well.
6. Incorporate the wet ingredients (including your chia mixture) into the dry and mix until well combined.
7. Shape into rounded scones and place on baking sheet. Bake for about 20 minutes, or until a toothpick inserted into the center comes out clean.
8. Remove from oven, let cool, and enjoy!

Per serving: Kcal 333; Carb 31g; Pro 10g; Fat 20g; Sat. Fat 2g; Fiber 8g; Omega-3 1.3; Sodium 280mg; Potassium 430mg; Magnesium 47mg; Vit D 11IU; Calcium 135mg; Iron 2.5mg

Zucchini Latkes with a Whipped Goat Cheese and Mint Sauce

Makes 3 servings

Ingredients:
- 2 large zucchinis, grated
- 2 tablespoons gluten-free flour (or whole-wheat flour)
- 1 large egg
- 1 tablespoon fresh thyme leaves
- 2 tablespoons olive oil
- 2 ounces goat cheese
- 1 tablespoon fresh lemon juice
- 1 tablespoon plain low-fat Greek yogurt
- 2 tablespoons mint, chopped
- Salt and pepper to taste

Directions:
1. Squeeze the water out of the grated zucchini and place in bowl.
2. Add flour, egg, thyme, salt, and pepper. Combine everything then form patties with your hands.
3. Heat olive oil on medium heat in a sauté pan.
4. Add 2 tablespoons zucchini mixture in sauté pan and let zucchini latke cook for 2 minutes.
5. Flip zucchini latke and allow it to brown on the other side, cooking for about 2 more minutes.
6. In a small bowl, combine goat cheese, lemon juice, Greek yogurt, mint, salt, and pepper.
7. Serve alongside zucchini latkes.

Per serving: Kcal 232; Carb 12g; Pro 10g; Fat 17g; Sat. Fat 6g; Fiber 1g; Omega-3 0.2g; Sodium 285mg; Potassium 644mg; Magnesium 57mg; Vit D 17IU; Calcium 142mg; Iron 2mg

Super Bowl Guacamole

Makes 8 servings

Ingredients:
- 4 ripe medium Hass avocados
- 2 jalapeño peppers, minced
- 1 shallot, minced
- ½ red onion, minced
- 2 tablespoons cilantro leaves, finely chopped
- 1 lime, juiced
- ½ teaspoon cumin
- Freshly ground black pepper and salt to taste

Directions:
1. Cut each avocado in half, twisting to open. Remove the seeds, scoop out the flesh into a bowl and mash with a fork. Set aside.
2. Mince the jalapeño, shallot, and red onion separately. Set aside.
3. In a bowl, mix all the ingredients until well combined, and enjoy!

Per serving: Kcal 122; Carb 8g; Pro 2g; Fat 10g; Sat. Fat 2g; Fiber 5g; Omega-3 0.1g; Sodium 37mg; Potassium 387mg; Magnesium 23mg; Vit D 0IU; Calcium 15mg; Iron 0.5mg

Creamed Spinach Artichoke Dip

THIS RECIPE CAN BE ENJOYED as a tasty dip, spread, or served warm as a "cream spinach" side. Melt mozzarella cheese (string cheese works too!) and put it on top of a piece of whole grain toast. Then top it all off with this dip with some sweet baby peppers on the side.

Makes 8 servings

Ingredients:
- 1 (16-ounce) bag frozen spinach
- 2 garlic cloves, minced
- ⅓ cup Trader Joe's vegan mayo
- ⅔ cup nonfat sour cream
- ½ cup parmesan cheese
- 1 (12-ounce) glass jar marinated artichokes
- 1 cup soft tofu
- ½ teaspoon onion powder
- ½ teaspoon cumin
- ¼ teaspoon paprika
- ½ teaspoon Bragg liquid aminos (or soy sauce)

Directions:
1. Defrost spinach in the microwave–you can use the defrost setting for two pounds.
2. Drain very well using a colander and press down with a large spoon to express all liquid.
3. Drain artichokes, but do not rinse.
4. Put all ingredients in a food processor and blend.
5. Enjoy!

Per serving: Kcal 180; Carb 13g; Pro 8g; Fat 12g; Sat. Fat 2g; Fiber 3g; Omega-3 0.1g; Sodium 380mg; Potassium 333mg; Magnesium 57mg; Vit D 1IU; Calcium 162mg; Iron 2mg

Brussels Sprouts

Makes 6 servings

Ingredients:
- 3 cups Brussels sprouts, sliced in halves
- 2 tablespoons olive oil

Traditional Taco Mix, makes around 1 tablespoon:
- ½ teaspoon corn starch
- ⅛ teaspoon sea salt
- ¼ teaspoon onion powder
- ½ teaspoon cumin
- ¼ teaspoon smoked paprika
- ½ teaspoon garlic powder
- ¼ teaspoon cayenne pepper
- ⅛ teaspoon sugar

Directions:
1. Mix your taco mix spices well in a small bowl and set aside.
2. Wash the Brussels sprouts and cut them in half.
3. Heat 2 tablespoons oil in a large pan, then add Brussels sprouts, cut side down.
4. Toss in 1 tablespoon taco mix and cook over medium heat for about 5-7 minutes.

Per serving: Kcal 62; Carb 5g; Pro 2g; Fat 5g; Sat. Fat 0.5g; Fiber 2g; Omega-3 0.1g; Sodium 52mg; Potassium 179mg; Magnesium 10mg; Vit D 0IU; Calcium 20mg; Iron 0.5mg

Crispy Sweet Potato Fries

Makes 4 servings

Ingredients:
- 2 pounds sweet potatoes
- 5 teaspoons olive oil

Choose one of the following seasonings:

Seasoning 1
- ⅓ teaspoon salt
- ¾ teaspoon black pepper

Seasoning 2
- ¾ teaspoon smoked paprika
- ⅓ teaspoon cumin
- ⅓ teaspoon garlic powder

Seasoning 3
- ⅓ teaspoon cinnamon
- 1½ teaspoons sugar
- 1 pinch salt

Directions:
1. Pre-heat oven to 400°F.
2. Slice sweet potatoes into 1-inch-long slices, then 1-inch-wide strips.
3. In a large bowl, toss sweet potatoes together with the olive oil.
4. Line a baking sheet with aluminum foil. Spread sweet potatoes in one single layer on the baking sheet.
5. Bake the sweet potatoes for about 25 minutes or until tender and golden brown.
6. Remove sweet potatoes from the oven and toss with spices.

Fries with Seasoning 1
Per serving: Kcal 246; Carb 46g; Pro 4g; Fat 6g; Sat. Fat 1g; Fiber 7g; Omega-3 0.1g; Sodium 285mg; Potassium 770mg; Magnesium 57mg; Vit D 0IU; Calcium 70mg; Iron 1mg

Fries with Seasoning 2
Per serving: Kcal 247; Carb 46g; Pro 4g; Fat 6g; Sat. Fat 1g; Fiber 7g; Omega-3 0.1g; Sodium 126mg; Potassium 777mg; Magnesium 58mg; Vit D 0IU; Calcium 70mg; Iron 2mg

Fries with Seasoning 3
Per serving: Kcal 251; Carb 47g; Pro 4g; Fat 6g; Sat. Fat 1g; Fiber 7g; Omega-3 0.1g; Sodium 185mg; Potassium 765mg; Magnesium 57mg; Vit D 0IU; Calcium 70mg; Iron 1mg

Strawberry Oat Scones

This scone recipe contains fewer added sugars and less saturated fat than your typical scone recipe, making it a perfect, less indulgent snack or treat. The scones are subtly sweet, so if you're in the mood for a little more sweetness, top with berry jam. They also pair well with tea or your favorite milk beverage.

Makes 8 scones (analysis based on 1 scone)

Ingredients:
- ½ cup cornmeal (buy finely ground or grind it with the oats when making the oat flour)
- 1 cup oat flour (you can make your own by grinding rolled oats in a coffee grinder)
- 1 cup whole-wheat flour
- 2 teaspoons cinnamon
- 1½ teaspoons baking powder
- ¼ teaspoon salt
- ¼ cup coconut flakes
- ½ cup honey
- 1 egg
- 1 cup sliced strawberries (either fresh or frozen)
- 4 tablespoons plain low-fat Greek yogurt
- ¼ cup olive oil

Add-ons: ½ cup dark chocolate chips

Per serving: Kcal 278; Carb 45g; Pro 5g; Fat 10g; Sat. Fat 3g; Fiber 5g; Omega-3 0.1g; Sodium 83mg; Potassium 148mg; Magnesium 59mg; Vit D 47IU; Calcium 147mg; Iron 2mg

Directions:
1. Preheat oven to 375°F.
2. In two separate bowls, mix the dry and wet ingredients.
3. Add the wet ingredients into the dry and mix until just incorporated.
4. Mold into your favorite scone shape and place on a lightly oiled cookie sheet.
5. Bake 20-25 minutes, or until cooked fully through. Remove from oven and cool.

Moroccan-Style Cauliflower

Makes 4 servings

Ingredients:

- ⅓ cup low-sodium vegetable broth or chicken broth
- 4 cups cauliflower florets
- 2 medium cloves garlic, minced
- ¼ teaspoon turmeric
- 2 tablespoons olive oil
- 1 tablespoon fresh lemon juice
- Salt and freshly ground black pepper
- 1½ tablespoons finely chopped fresh cilantro

Directions:

1. Pour broth in large skillet over medium-high heat.
2. When broth begins to steam, add cauliflower, garlic, and turmeric.
3. Stir to combine and cover.
4. Cook cauliflower for 4-5 minutes for al dente, or 5-6 minutes for more tender.
5. Remove skillet from heat and transfer cauliflower mixture into a medium bowl.
6. Add oil, lemon juice, and salt and pepper to taste.
7. Gently toss to combine well, then sprinkle on the cilantro and gently toss again.
8. Serve warm or at room temperature.

Per serving: Kcal 92; Carb 7g; Pro 2g; Fat 7g; Sat. Fat 1g; Fiber 2g; Omega-3 0g; Sodium 163mg; Potassium 337mg; Magnesium 17mg; Vit D 0IU; Calcium 29mg; Iron 1mg

Spiced Sweet Potato Sauté

THIS SPICED SWEET POTATO DISH is loaded with warm Indian inspired flavors. It is also very versatile! You can pair it with your favorite whole grain, use as a wrap or omelet filling, or mix it into a green salad. It also tastes great mixed with your favorite type of beans. This recipe is sure to warm you up from the inside out!

Makes 6 servings

Ingredients:
- 3 large sweet potatoes, sliced ½-inch thick
- 2 tablespoons olive oil
- 1 teaspoon turmeric
- 1 teaspoon chopped jalapeño, seeds and rib removed
- 1 cup tomato, chopped
- 1 teaspoon cumin seeds
- 1 teaspoon ginger root, chopped
- ¼ cup chopped cilantro
- ⅔ cup water
- Salt to taste

Directions:
1. In a large skillet, heat olive oil on medium heat.
2. Add turmeric and cumin seeds and let toast for 30 seconds, making sure not to burn them.
3. Add the sliced sweet potatoes and ⅓ cup water. Cover with a lid, and sauté for 8-10 minutes, stirring occasionally.
4. Add salt, tomatoes, jalapeños, ginger, and another ⅓ cup water.
5. Cover again and cook for an additional 8-10 minutes on low-to-medium heat, stirring occasionally.
6. Once sweet potatoes are tender, garnish with chopped cilantro and enjoy!

Per serving: Kcal 104; Carb 15g; Pro 2g; Fat 5g; Sat. Fat 1g; Fiber 2g; Omega-3 0g; Sodium 78mg; Potassium 308mg; Magnesium 22mg; Vit D 0IU; Calcium 27mg; Iron 1mg

Turmeric Yogurt Dip

Makes 4 servings

Ingredients:
- 1 cup plain low-fat Greek yogurt
- 1 tablespoon olive oil
- ½ cup basil leaves
- 1 tablespoon tahini paste
- ½ teaspoon turmeric
- Salt and pepper to taste

Directions:
1. In a food processor add the yogurt, tahini, turmeric, basil, olive oil, salt and pepper. Blend until smooth.
2. Serve with vegetable crudité or pita chips.

Per serving: Kcal 99; Carb 4g; Pro 7g; Fat 7g; Sat. Fat 1.5g; Fiber 0g; Omega-3 0g; Sodium 83mg; Potassium 126mg; Magnesium 15mg; Vit D 0IU; Calcium 86mg; Iron 0.5mg

Cumin Cucumber Rice Cake

Makes 1 rice cake

Ingredients:
- 1 brown rice cake
- 2 tablespoons hummus
- ⅛ cup chopped cucumber
- ⅛ teaspoon cumin

Directions:
1. Chop cucumber into small bite-sized pieces.
2. Spread hummus on rice cake.
3. Add cucumber.
4. Sprinkle with cumin.

Per serving: Kcal 143; Carb 26g; Pro 4g; Fat 4g; Sat. Fat 1 g; Fiber 2g; Omega-3 0g; Sodium 316mg; Potassium 19mg; Magnesium 2mg; Vit D 0IU; Calcium 24mg; Iron 2mg

Fig & Raspberry Ricotta Rice Cake

Makes 1 rice cake

Ingredients:
- 1 brown rice cake
- 4 tablespoons part-skim ricotta cheese
- 2 teaspoons raspberry jam
- ½ teaspoon cocoa
- 4 small dried figs, chopped

Directions:
1. Mix ricotta, raspberry jam, and cocoa together in a small bowl.
2. Spread the mixture onto the brown rice cake.
3. Slice the dried figs, place them on top of the ricotta mix, and enjoy!

Per serving: Kcal 248; Carb 43g; Pro 9g; Fat 6g; Sat. Fat 3g; Fiber 5g; Omega-3 0g; Sodium 101mg; Potassium 306mg; Magnesium 32mg; Vit D 4IU; Calcium 243mg; Iron 2mg

Tahini Chocolate Rice Cake

Makes 1 rice cake

Ingredients:
- 1 brown rice cake
- 1 tablespoon tahini
- ½ teaspoon unsweetened cocoa powder
- 6 raspberries (or more)
- 1 square dark chocolate pieces, broken (65% dark chocolate)

Directions:
1. Spread the tahini on your rice cake.
2. Dust with the cocoa powder.
3. Top with raspberries and broken dark chocolate pieces.

Per serving: Kcal 204; Carb 24g; Pro 5g; Fat 12g; Sat. Fat 3g; Fiber 4g; Omega-3 0.1g; Sodium 40mg; Potassium 89mg; Magnesium 18mg; Vit D 0IU; Calcium 24mg; Iron 2mg

Salted Amaranth Cornbread

Makes 9 servings

Ingredients:
- 1½ cups organic cornmeal
- ½ cup amaranth flour
- ¼ cup white sugar
- ½ teaspoon baking powder
- ½ teaspoon baking soda
- ½ teaspoon salt
- 1 egg, beaten
- 5 ounces plain nonfat Greek yogurt
- ½ cup low-fat sour cream
- ⅓ cup skim milk
- ⅛ cup butter, melted
- ½ teaspoon sea salt

Directions:
1. Preheat oven to 400°F.
2. Spray or use olive oil to lightly coat an 8" x 8" baking dish.
3. In a large bowl, mix together the cornmeal, amaranth flour, sugar, baking powder, baking soda, and salt, then set aside.
4. In a small bowl, beat egg, then add Greek yogurt, sour cream, milk, and melted butter.
5. Fold wet ingredients into dry ingredients, mixing until just incorporated.
6. Transfer batter into prepared pan and bake for 20-25 minutes.
7. Remove from oven when surface of cornbread is golden-brown, and a toothpick inserted into the center comes out clean.
8. Lightly sprinkle with sea salt, serve, and enjoy!

Per serving: Kcal 175; Carb 28g; Pro 6g; Fat 5g; Sat. Fat 2g; Fiber 2g; Omega-3 0.1g; Sodium 386mg; Potassium 97mg; Magnesium 37mg; Vit D 8IU; Calcium 102mg; Iron 1mg

Creamy Coleslaw

Makes 2 servings

Ingredients:

- 1 bag (~10 ounces) prewashed, ready-made chopped veggies, like broccoli slaw, organic coleslaw or my favorite, kale, cabbage, and shaved Brussels sprouts slaw
- 4-5 tablespoons plain nonfat Greek yogurt
- 2 tablespoons vegan mayonnaise
- 1 teaspoon white balsamic vinegar
- 1 teaspoon honey
- 1 dash chili lime seasoning
- 1 dash smoked paprika

Add-on: 1 teaspoon spicy brown or yellow mustard, salt and pepper to taste

Per serving: Kcal 162; Carb 13g; Pro 7g; Fat 10g; Sat. Fat 1g; Fiber 4g; Omega-3 0g; Sodium 140mg; Potassium 34mg; Magnesium 0mg; Vit D 0IU; Calcium 102mg; Iron 1.5mg

Directions:

1. Mix Greek yogurt, mayonnaise, vinegar, honey, and spices in a large bowl. You can use any herb/spice combination you like. Have fun experimenting!
2. Add the veggie slaw mixture.
3. Mix and toss with 2 large spoons until evenly coated.

Ginger Turmeric Lime Smoothie

Makes 1 serving

Ingredients:

- 4-inch piece fresh ginger root, peeled
- 2-inch piece (4.4g) fresh turmeric root, peeled
- 8 ounces filtered water
- 1 scoop (~27g) vanilla whey protein powder (or pea protein powder)
- 1 small Fuji apple, diced
- 1½ cups pre-washed kale, chopped
- 1 whole lime, peeled and cut in 4 parts
- A few ice cubes

Per serving: Kcal 262; Carb 47g; Pro 21g; Fat 2g; Sat. Fat 1g; Fiber 8g; Omega-3 0g Sodium 97mg; Potassium 427mg; Magnesium 25mg; Vit D 0IU; Calcium 292mg; Iron 3mg

Directions:

1. Juice the ginger and turmeric root.
2. Add juice and all remaining ingredients into a blender and puree until smooth.

Tofu Nuggets

Makes 5 servings

Ingredients for Hoisin Sauce:
- 3 tablespoons Bragg liquid aminos (or soy sauce – not GF)
- 1 teaspoon spicy sesame oil
- 1 teaspoon GF hoisin sauce (labeled for barbecue stir-fry)
- 1 teaspoon honey
- ¼ teaspoon dried garlic powder
- ¼ teaspoon fresh garlic, minced

Other Ingredients:
- 1 (16-ounce) package pressed or firm tofu (pressed tofu has the water drained and is very firm)
- ⅓ cup cornmeal
- ⅓ cup oat flour
- ⅛ teaspoon cumin
- ⅛ teaspoon garlic powder
- ⅛ teaspoon paprika
- Oil for baking pan

Directions:
1. After pressing the tofu to remove any excess liquid, slice the tofu block horizontally into 1-inch-thick rectangles, then slice into bite-sized rectangles or squares.
2. Mix all sauce ingredients together. Save a third of the sauce for dipping and use the remaining sauce to marinate the tofu for 10 minutes (or for up to 1 hour in the fridge).
3. Preheat oven to 375°F. Lightly coat a baking sheet with oil or use a silicone mat to prevent sticking.
4. In a large bowl, mix together cornmeal, oat flour, cumin, garlic, and paprika.
5. Remove tofu from the marinade, pat into flour mixture on both sides, then place breaded tofu on a baking sheet.
6. Bake for 8 minutes, flip and bake for 5 more minutes or until golden brown.

If you're concerned about genetically modified foods, purchase non-GMO or organic tofu.

Recipe (without oil for pan)
Per serving: Kcal 155; Carb 15g; Pro 11g; Fat 6g; Sat. Fat 1g; Fiber 2g; Omega-3 0g; Sodium 625mg; Potassium 84mg; Magnesium 15mg; Vit D 0IU; Calcium 121mg; Iron 2mg

Snacks/Sides

Apple & Peanut Butter with Whey Shake

Makes 1 serving

Ingredients:

Whey Shake
- 1 scoop vanilla whey protein powder
- ½ cup water
- ½ cup skim milk
- ½ medium banana

Apple & PB
- 1 medium apple
- 1 tablespoon peanut butter (or nut butter of your choice)

Directions:
1. In a blender combine all whey shake ingredients and serve.
2. Slice apple.
3. Top each piece with the nut butter of your choice.

Whey Shake
Per serving: Kcal 204; Carb 26g; Pro 22g; Fat 2g; Sat. Fat 1g; Fiber 2g; Omega-3 0g; Sodium 97mg; Potassium 532mg; Magnesium 45mg; Vit D 57IU; Calcium 253mg; Iron 0mg

Apple & PB
Per serving: Kcal 190; Carb 29g; Pro 4g; Fat 9g; Sat. Fat 2g; Fiber 5g; Omega-3 0g; Sodium 70mg; Potassium 284mg; Magnesium 36mg; Vit D 0IU; Calcium 19mg; Iron 1mg

Edamame Greek Yogurt Dip

This protein-packed edamame Greek yogurt dip makes the perfect refreshing snack. Meyer lemon and fresh herbs impart fresh flavors to help liven up your day. Pair with fresh veggies or your favorite whole grain crackers. Add ½ avocado for extra creaminess and to boost those heart-healthy unsaturated fats. This also makes the perfect appetizer to bring along to your next potluck!

Makes 4 servings

Ingredients:

- 2½ tablespoons lemon juice (zest from ~1 Meyer lemon)
- 1 garlic clove
- 1 teaspoon cumin
- 1 cup shelled edamame
- 1 cup plain nonfat Greek yogurt
- 8-10 leaves fresh basil
- 4 sprigs fresh dill
- 2 tablespoons olive oil
- Salt and pepper to taste
- Dash of chili powder

Add-on: ½ small Hass avocado

Per serving: Kcal 146; Carb 8g; Pro 10g; Fat 9g; Sat. Fat 1g; Fiber 2g; Omega-3 0g; Sodium 109mg; Potassium 79mg; Magnesium 2mg; Vit D 0IU; Calcium 96mg; Iron 1mg

Directions:

1. In a blender or food processor, combine all ingredients except olive oil, salt, pepper, and chili powder. Blend until smooth.
2. Stir in olive oil and remaining spices, then transfer into a serving bowl.
3. Serve with a side of veggies.

Tangy and Savory Greek Yogurt Dip

Enjoy Greek yogurt dip as a savory snack or with a meal as a dressing. Experiment in the kitchen to make your own favorite dips! Try mixing a small amount of yogurt with a sprinkle of your favorite herbs and discover what you like best.

Makes 2 servings

Ingredients:
- ⅔ cup plain 2% Greek yogurt
- ½ cup light sour cream (or replace with Greek yogurt)
- 1 tablespoon Meyer lemon juice
- ¼ teaspoon onion powder
- ¼ teaspoon garlic powder
- ⅛ teaspoon salt
- ⅛ teaspoon coriander seeds
- ½ teaspoon fresh ground pepper
- 2 tablespoons dill leaves –pressed into tablespoon
- 2 teaspoons thyme leaves –pressed into teaspoon
- Additional salt and pepper to taste

Directions:
1. Wash and juice lemon.
2. Place all ingredients in blender or food processor and mix.

Per serving: Kcal 283; Carb 15g; Pro 11g; Fat 3g; Sat. Fat 1.5g; Fiber 0g; Omega-3 0g; Sodium 218mg; Potassium 283mg; Magnesium 14mg; Vit D 0IU; Calcium 187mg; Iron 0mg

Roasted Honey Drizzled Beets

ROASTED BEETS MAKE A DELICIOUS side dish or hearty snack and have tons of health benefits. Add some beets to your day with this easy, sweet and earthy recipe.

Makes 2 servings

Ingredients:
- 3 small-to-medium beets (about 2 inches in size)
- 1½ tablespoons olive oil
- 2 teaspoons honey
- Salt and pepper to taste

Add-ons: Dried thyme, basil, or oregano

Directions:
1. Preheat oven to 400°F.
2. Wash and scrub the beets, rub with olive oil, wrap tightly in aluminum foil, and place on a baking sheet.
3. Place in oven and allow beets to roast for about one hour, or until soft and tender in the center.
4. Remove from oven when tender, then allow to cool.
5. In a small saucepan, over medium heat, warm the honey, olive oil, and your choice of herbs, for a couple minutes.
6. Slice beets into bite-sized wedges, place in a bowl, drizzle warmed honey mixture, and stir well.
7. Enjoy!

Per serving: Kcal 162; Carb 17g; Pro 2g; Fat 11g; Sat. Fat 2g; Fiber 3g; Omega-3 0g; Sodium 242mg; Potassium 400mg; Magnesium 28mg; Vit D 0IU; Calcium 20mg; Iron 1mg

Stuffed Dates Three Ways

BUILD YOUR OWN STUFFED DATES! These are simple and tasty bites that can satisfy a sugar craving or hold you over to your next meal! Medjool dates are nature's true candy, extra caramelly and sweet. For the vegan option, make sure your chocolate chips don't contain milk.

Makes 1 serving

Ingredients:

Base: 2 Medjool dates

Stuffing Options:
- Option 1: 5 semi-sweet chocolate chips (or dark chocolate)
- Option 2: 1 teaspoon crunchy (or smooth) peanut butter
- Option 3: 4 walnuts halves

Directions:

1. Remove the pit from the dates.
2. Choose one stuffing option or mix and match two different ones!

2 Medjool dates
Kcal 133; Carb 36g; Pro 1g; Fat 0g; Sat. Fat 0g; Fiber 3g; Omega-3 0g; Sodium 0mg; Potassium 334mg; Magnesium 26mg; Vit D 0IU; Calcium 31mg; Iron 0.5mg

Option 1
5 semi-sweet chocolate chips
Kcal 11; Carb 2g; Pro 0g; Fat 1g; Sat. Fat 0.5g; Fiber 0g; Omega-3 0g; Sodium 0mg; Potassium 9mg; Magnesium 3mg; Vit D 0IU; Calcium 1mg; Iron 0mg

Option 2
1 teaspoon crunchy peanut butter
Kcal 31; Carb 1g; Pro 1g; Fat 3g; Sat. Fat 0.5g; Fiber 0g; Omega-3 0g; Sodium 26mg; Potassium 40mg; Magnesium 9mg; Vit D 0IU; Calcium 2mg; Iron 0mg

Option 3
4 walnut halves
Kcal 52; Carb 1g; Pro 1g; Fat 5g; Sat. Fat 0.5g; Fiber 1g; Omega-3 0.7g; Sodium 0mg; Potassium 35mg; Magnesium 13mg; Vit D 0IU; Calcium 8mg; Iron 0mg

DESSERTS

Maple Cocoa Brownie

Makes 5 brownies (analysis based on 1 brownie)

Ingredients:
- ½ cup sweet potato, peeled, steamed
- ¼ cup smooth peanut butter
- ¼ cup maple syrup
- 1 egg
- ¾ cup chickpea flour
- ½ teaspoon baking soda
- ½ teaspoon cinnamon
- ¼ cup raw unsweetened cacao (or cocoa)
- ¼ teaspoon salt

Directions:
1. Preheat oven to 350°F.
2. In a large mixing bowl combine sweet potato, peanut butter, maple syrup and egg. Mix until ingredients are well blended.
3. In a different mixing bowl combine the dry ingredients: chickpea flour, cinnamon, baking soda, raw cacao and salt.
4. In small increments at a time add dry ingredients to wet ingredients until fully mixed together.
5. Line an 8" x 8" baking dish with wax paper.
6. Spread the mixture evenly over wax paper in baking dish.
7. Bake at 350°F for 20 minutes.
8. After 20 minutes, a toothpick inserted in the brownies should come out clean.
9. Let cool fully, slice, and enjoy!

Per serving: Kcal 224; Carb 28g; Pro 7g; Fat 10g; Sat. Fat 2g; Fiber 3g; Omega-3 0g; Sodium 354mg; Potassium 365mg; Magnesium 53mg; Vit D 7IU; Calcium 49mg; Iron 1mg

Date These Brownies

WHO THOUGHT YOU'D EVER SEE a recipe with black beans and pea protein in the ingredients for brownies?! While this may sound like an interesting combination, it's actually a delicious pairing. These brownies will boost your protein intake and fulfill that dessert craving, all in one! They're more of a healthy treat than a truly indulgent one, so you can enjoy them a little more often than you would the more traditional brownie recipe.

Makes 10 brownies (analysis based on 1 brownie)

Ingredients:
- 1 (15-ounce) can whole black beans, drained and rinsed
- ½ cup maple syrup
- 2 eggs
- ¼ cup vegetable oil
- 1 medium banana
- 5 large Medjool dates
- ½ cup unsweetened cocoa powder
- ¼ cup unsweetened almond milk
- ½ cup oats
- 2 tablespoons (29g) unsweetened pea protein powder
- 1 teaspoon vanilla extract
- ¼ teaspoon salt
- ½ teaspoon baking powder
- ¼ cup dark chocolate chips

Directions:
1. Preheat oven to 350°F and lightly oil a baking pan.
2. Combine all ingredients except dark chocolate chips in a food processor or blender, and blend until well mixed.
3. Pour into a baking pan, stir in dark chocolate chips, and bake for about 30-35 minutes, or until center is fully set.
4. Remove from oven and let cool.
5. Enjoy with some flavored Greek yogurt for an added touch of sweetness and protein.

Per serving: Kcal 252; Carb 35g; Pro 8g; Fat 9g; Sat. Fat 2g; Fiber 6g; Omega-3 0g; Sodium 131mg; Potassium 295mg; Magnesium 17mg; Vit D 10IU; Calcium 87mg; Iron 4mg

Cocoa Chia Pudding

ANT TO CUT DOWN ON added sugars? Try this recipe without the sweetener and use berries instead! See what you think! If it's too bitter, you can always add in the sweetener at the end.

Makes 1 serving

Ingredients:
- 3 tablespoons chia seeds
- 1 cup unsweetened almond milk (or your choice of milk)
- 1 tablespoon unsweetened cocoa powder
- 1½ teaspoons honey (or maple syrup or agave)

Add-ons: Scoop of yogurt, vanilla extract, cinnamon, fresh or frozen berries, or your favorite nuts or seeds

Directions:
1. Combine all ingredients together in a jar, large mug, or bowl and mix well.
2. Let sit for at least 15 minutes. The longer you wait, the more pudding-like it becomes.

Per serving: Kcal 237; Carb 27g; Pro 8g; Fat 13g; Sat. Fat 1g; Fiber 13g; Omega-3 5.6g; Sodium 193mg; Potassium 391mg; Magnesium 151mg; Vit D 110IU; Calcium 722mg; Iron 4mg

Lemony Blackberry Chia Pudding

Makes 3-4 servings (analysis based on 4 servings)

Ingredients:
- 1 cup 2% DHA fortified milk
- 1 (5.6-ounce) container flavored Greek yogurt (we used mango)
- 4 tablespoons nonfat plain Greek yogurt
- 2 teaspoons maple syrup
- 1 teaspoon vanilla extract
- ½ teaspoon lemon zest
- ¼ cup chia seeds
- 1 cup blackberries (fresh or frozen)

Directions:
1. Whisk milk, yogurt, maple syrup, vanilla extract, and lemon zest together.
2. Add in chia seeds and whisk well again.
3. Cover tightly and place in the refrigerator.
4. Add in blackberries in the morning and serve.

Per serving: Kcal 172; Carb 21g; Pro 10g; Fat 6g; Sat. Fat 1g; Fiber 8g; Omega-3 3g; Sodium 95mg; Potassium 225mg; Magnesium 8mg; Vit D 41IU; Calcium 225mg; Iron 1mg

Graham Cracker Dessert

Makes 1 serving

Ingredients:
- 1 tablespoon almond butter
- 1 tablespoon dark chocolate chips
- 2 graham cracker sheets

Directions:
1. In small bowl add 1 tablespoon almond butter and 1 tablespoon dark chocolate chips, and heat in the microwave 20-30 seconds.
2. Mix well, then top graham crackers with the mixture.
3. Use any leftover dark chocolate chips as a topping for each graham cracker.

Per serving: Kcal 299; Carb 33g; Pro 6g; Fat 16g; Sat. Fat 4.5g; Fiber 4g; Omega-3 0.2g; Sodium 165mg; Potassium 167mg; Magnesium 56mg; Vit D 0IU; Calcium 77mg; Iron 2.5mg

Honey Bee Peanut Butter Cookies

MADE WITH PEANUT BUTTER, WHOLE-WHEAT flour, and light on added sugar, these cookies make the perfect healthy treat. I love them warm and paired with a glass of tea. They are nutty, just the right amount of sweet, and perfectly crumbly!

Makes about 30 cookies (analysis based on 1 cookie)

Ingredients:
- 1¾ cups whole-wheat flour
- 1 teaspoon baking soda
- ¼ teaspoon salt
- 1 teaspoon cinnamon
- 1½ cups peanut butter (my favorite is chunky!)
- ½ cup honey (or sweetener of choice)
- ¼ cup unsweetened almond milk
- 2 tablespoons olive oil

Add-ons: Coconut flakes, dark chocolate chips, 1 teaspoon vanilla extract

Directions:
1. Preheat oven to 350°F.
2. Mix wet and dry ingredients separately, then add the dry ingredients into the wet and mix until just incorporated. Scoop by the tablespoon onto an oiled baking sheet, then press down with the back of a fork to make a crisscross pattern.
3. Bake for about 9 minutes, keeping a close eye because they can burn quickly!
4. Remove from oven, let sit for a few minutes, then transfer to a cooling rack.

Per serving: Kcal 126; Carb 13g; Pro 4g; Fat 8g; Sat. Fat 1g; Fiber 1g; Omega-3 0g; Sodium 114mg; Potassium 102mg; Magnesium 31mg; Vit D 1IU; Calcium 14mg; Iron 1mg

Whey Protein Peanut Butter Cookies

THIS IS ONE OF MY favorite cookie recipes. The peanut butter and whole-wheat flour offer a perfect flavor balance with the added whey protein. The added whey will also help boost your protein intake.

Makes about 30 cookies (analysis based on 1 cookie)

Ingredients:
- 1¾ cups whole-wheat flour
- 1 teaspoon baking soda
- ⅔ cup whey protein
- ¼ teaspoon salt
- 1 teaspoon cinnamon
- 1½ cups peanut butter (my favorite is chunky!)
- ½ cup honey or sweetener of choice
- ½ cup + 2 tablespoons unsweetened almond milk
- 2 tablespoons olive oil

Add-ons: 1 teaspoon vanilla extract, coconut flakes, or dark chocolate chips

Directions:
1. Preheat oven to 350°F.
2. Mix wet and dry ingredients separately, then add the dry ingredients into the wet and mix until just incorporated.
3. Scoop with a tablespoon onto an oiled baking sheet, then press down with the back of a fork to make a crisscross pattern.
4. Bake for about 8 minutes, keeping a close eye because they can burn quickly!
5. Remove from oven, let sit for a few minutes, then transfer to a cooling rack.

Per serving: Kcal 141; Carb 12g; Pro 5g; Fat 8g; Sat. Fat 1g; Fiber 2g; Omega-3 0g; Sodium 104mg; Potassium 38mg; Magnesium 11mg; Vit D 2IU; Calcium 21mg; Iron 0mg

Sweet & Savory Pumpkin Bowl

Makes 2 servings

Ingredients:

- 1 cup canned pumpkin (or pumpkin puree)
- 1 medium Fuji apple, chopped
- ½ cup nonfat Greek yogurt
- 8 walnuts
- 1 teaspoon maple syrup
- ¼ teaspoon vanilla extract
- ⅛ teaspoon cinnamon

Directions:

1. Wash and chop apple into small squares and microwave for 2 minutes.
2. Rinse off the top of the can of pumpkin and open.
3. Place 1 cup pumpkin in the bowl with apple, cover with silicon cover or waxed paper, and microwave for 1 minute.
4. Add in yogurt, walnuts, vanilla extract and cinnamon, and mix.
5. Top with maple syrup.

Per serving: Kcal 243; Carb 29g; Pro 9g; Fat 11g; Sat. Fat 1g; Fiber 6g; Omega-3 1.4g; Sodium 27mg; Potassium 236mg; Magnesium 31mg; Vit D 0IU; Calcium 109mg; Iron 2mg

Blueberry Acai Dessert

Makes 1-2 servings (analysis based on 2 servings)

Ingredients:
- 1 (5-ounce) pack frozen, sweetened Acai
- ½ cup frozen blueberries
- 1 tablespoon water

Directions:
1. Run frozen Acai pack under hot/warm water, just enough to break it down to put into the food processor.
2. Add all ingredients into a food processor and blend until well combined.

Per serving: Kcal 98; Carb 15g; Pro 1g; Fat 3g; Sat. Fat 1g; Fiber 2g; Omega-3 0g; Sodium 6mg; Potassium 21mg; Magnesium 2mg; Vit D 0IU; Calcium 31mg; Iron 1mg

Chocolate Drizzled Apples

Makes 1 serving

Ingredients:
- 1 medium apple, cut into wedges
- 1½ tablespoons peanut butter
- 2 tablespoons dark chocolate chips
- 1 tablespoon unsweetened dried coconut

Directions:
1. Slice apple into wedges.
2. Drizzle with peanut butter.
3. Top with coconut flakes and chocolate. You can melt the chocolate quickly in the microwave and drizzle it instead, for an added touch!

Per serving: Kcal 385; Carb 43g; Pro 7g; Fat 23g; Sat. Fat 10g; Fiber 8g; Omega-3 0g; Sodium 105mg; Potassium 329mg; Magnesium 49mg; Vit D 0IU; Calcium 23mg; Iron 3mg

Chocolate Chip Oat Protein Bites

 NJOY THESE PROTEIN BITES STRAIGHT out of the freezer. They are both soft and crunchy – the perfect texture!

Makes 18 bites (analysis based on 1 bite)

Ingredients:
- ½ cup + ⅓ cup oats
- ⅛ cup flax meal
- 3 tablespoons almond butter
- 2 scoops (30g) vanilla whey protein (contains stevia)
- 1 scoop (25g) regular whey protein
- ½ teaspoon vanilla extract
- ¼ teaspoon cinnamon
- 2 tablespoons maple syrup
- ⅓ cup semi-sweet chocolate chips
- 1 medium apple, finely shredded

Directions:
1. Preheat the oven to 300°F.
2. Mix ½ cup oats, flax meal, almond butter, protein powders, vanilla extract, cinnamon, maple syrup, and semi-sweet chocolate chips in a large bowl.
3. Stir in the shredded apple until mixture is runny.
4. Fold in remaining ⅓ cup oats.
5. Use a tablespoon to scoop and roll into balls. Keep a bowl of cold water close by to use if the mixture sticks to your hands.
6. Place on a cookie sheet covered with a silicon baking mat or parchment paper.
7. Bake at 300°F for 10 minutes.
8. Flip balls over and continue cooking for another 2 minutes or until golden brown. If you flip too early, the balls will lose their shape and the chocolate will run out of the cookie.
9. Let balls cool, then place in freezer.

Per serving: Kcal 98; Carb 10g; Pro 5g; Fat 4g; Sat. Fat 1g; Fiber 2g; Omega-3 0g; Sodium 13mg; Potassium 54mg; Magnesium 10mg; Vit D 0IU; Calcium 30mg; Iron 1mg

Tiger Nut Flour Donuts

This recipe is very versatile and keeps things interesting! Bake in a donut tin for donuts, cook in a waffle iron for waffles, bake in a muffin tin for muffins, or drizzle on the griddle for pancakes! The options are endless! Use coconut oil spray for a flavor boost.

Makes 12 donuts (analysis based on 1 donut)

Ingredients:

- 1¾ cups oat flour
- ½ cup tiger nut flour
- 4 teaspoons baking powder
- 1 teaspoon guar gum
- ¼ teaspoon salt
- ½ teaspoon cinnamon
- ⅛ teaspoon nutmeg
- 4 teaspoons sugar
- 3 eggs
- 3 medium bananas, mashed
- 1⅓ cups unsweetened soy milk
- ¼ cup canola oil – if concerned about GMOs, purchase non-GMO or organic canola oil
- 1 teaspoon natural vanilla extract
- 1 cup crushed walnuts

Directions:

1. Preheat oven to 350°F.
2. Mix the oat flour, tiger nut flour, baking powder, guar gum, salt, cinnamon, nutmeg, and sugar in a large bowl.
3. Whisk eggs in a separate bowl.
4. Mix the bananas, soy milk, canola oil, and vanilla extract into the whisked eggs.
5. Stir wet ingredients into the dry ingredients.
6. Add walnuts and stir until batter is smooth.
7. Lightly coat your pan with oil, then fill your donut tin close to the top.
8. Bake for about 20 minutes, or until a toothpick comes out clean.
9. Top with your choice of fruit, yogurt, walnuts, cinnamon and/or syrup.

Per serving: Kcal 245; Carb 23g; Pro 7g; Fat 15g; Sat. Fat 2g; Fiber 5g; Omega-3 0.9g; Sodium 68mg; Potassium 247mg; Magnesium 75mg; Vit D 9IU; Calcium 239mg; Iron 2mg

*Omega-3 and Vit D content not available for tigernut flour

www.ingramcontent.com/pod-product-compliance
Lightning Source LLC
Chambersburg PA
CBHW061149070526
44584CB00034B/4463